KAWAII

COLORING BOOK

THIS BOOK BELONGS TO:

____

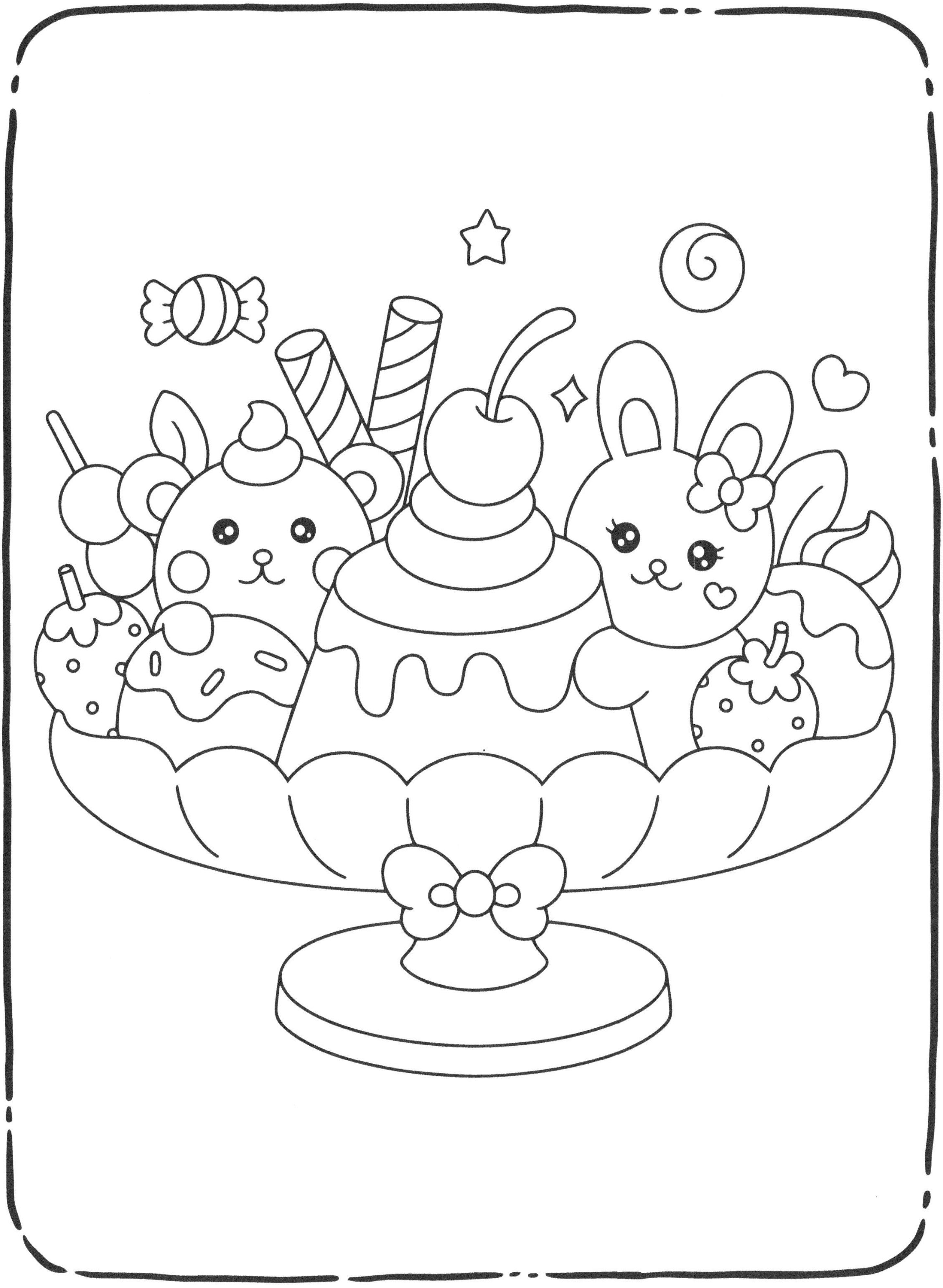

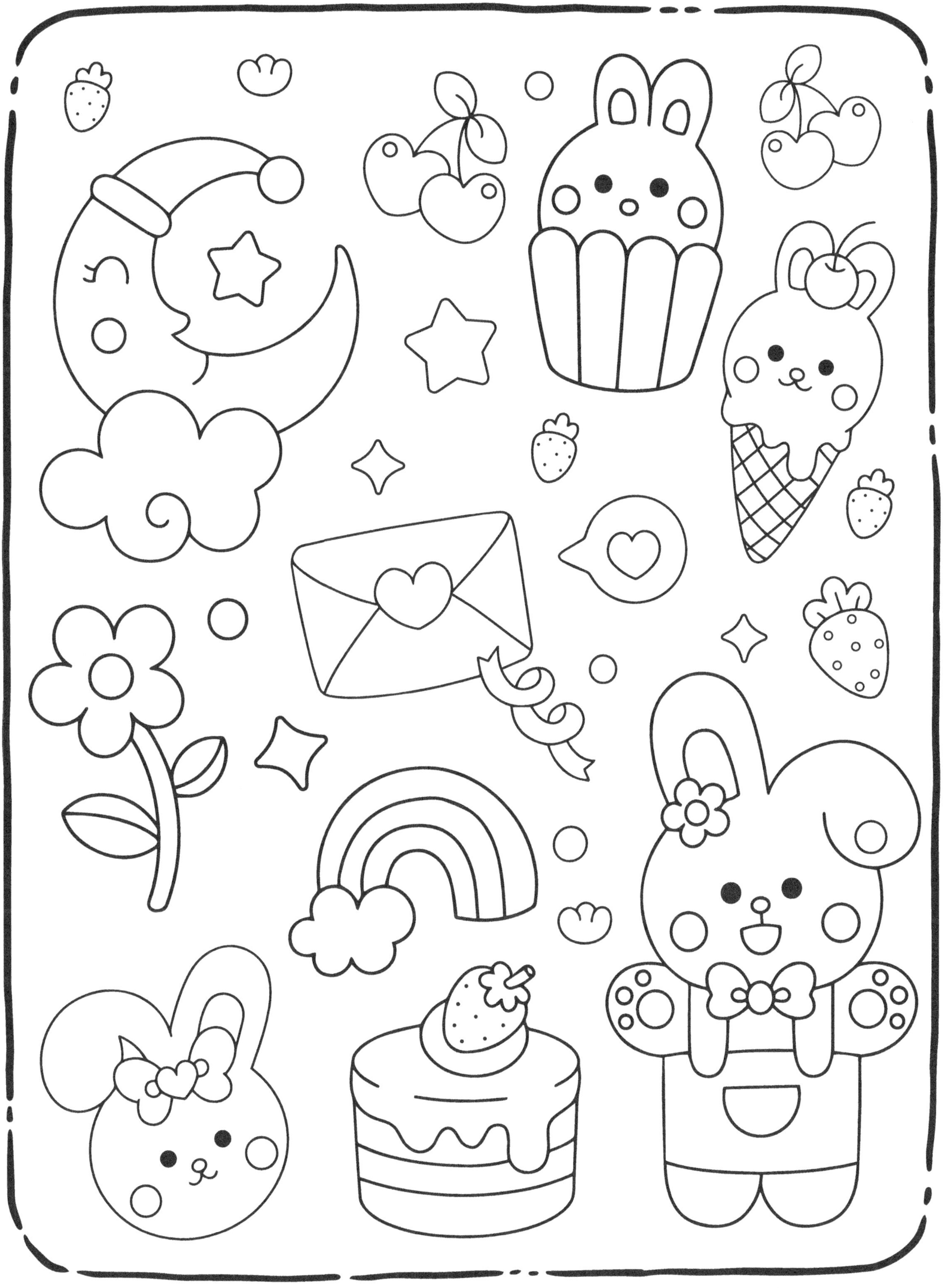

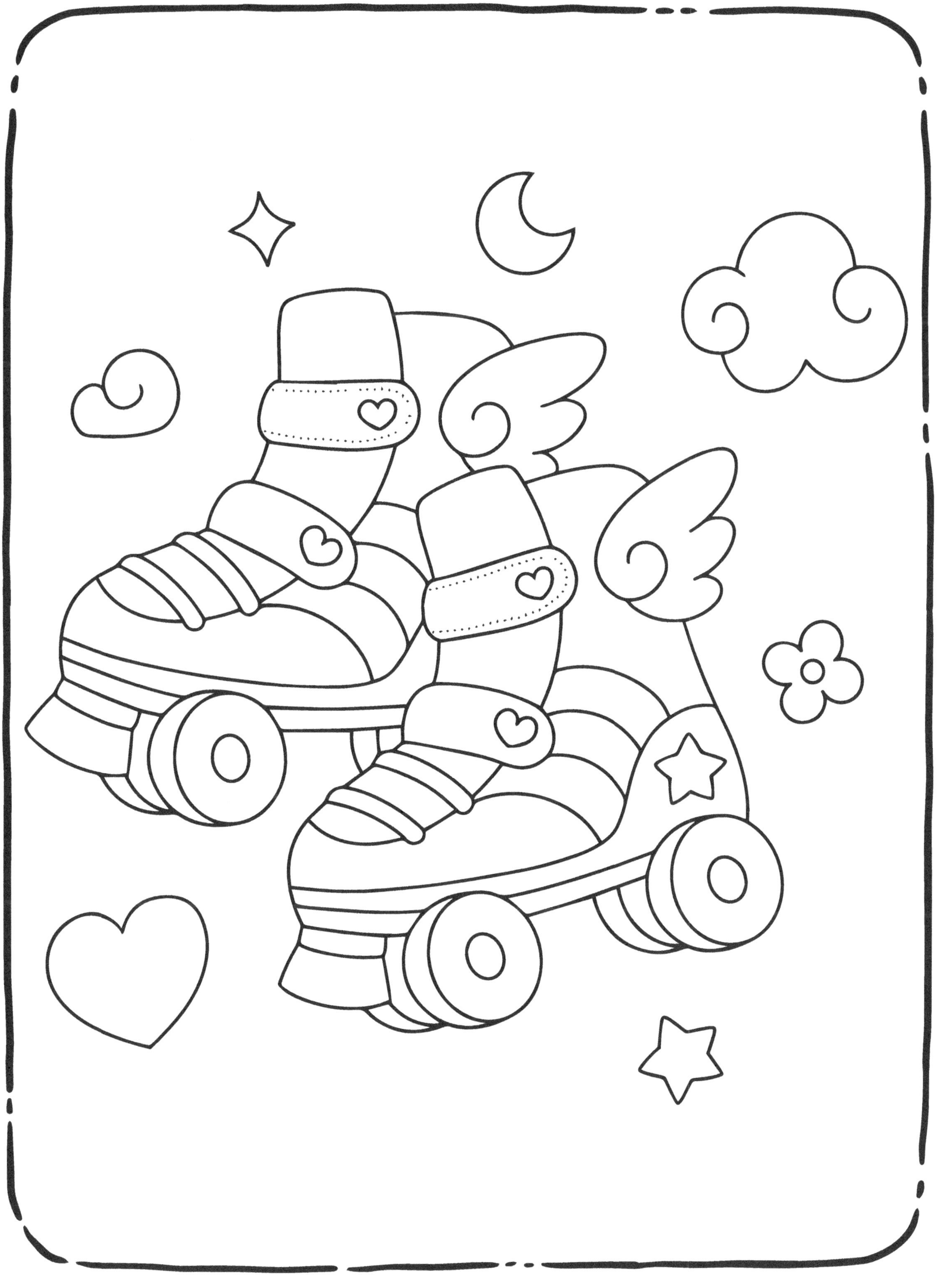

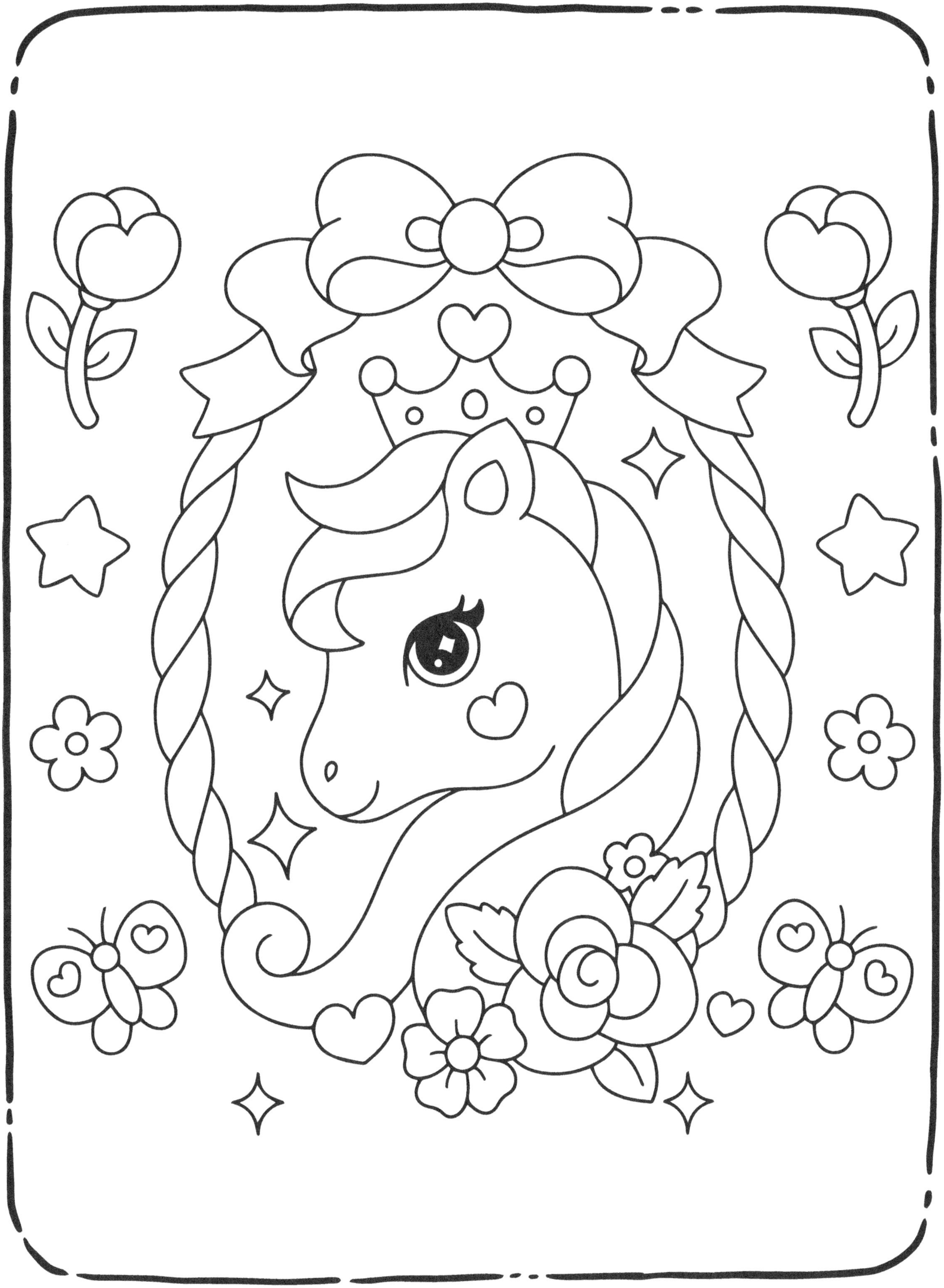

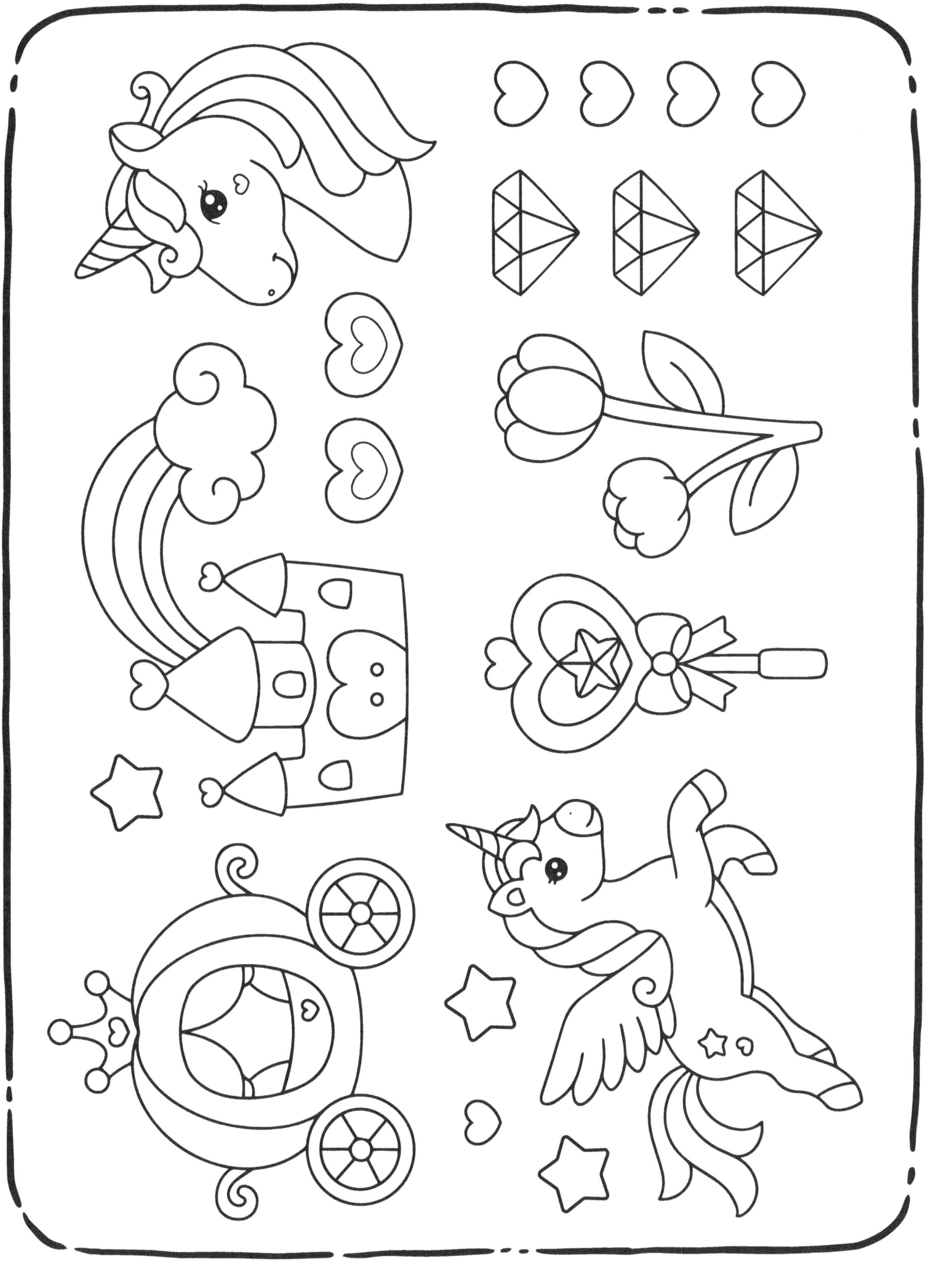

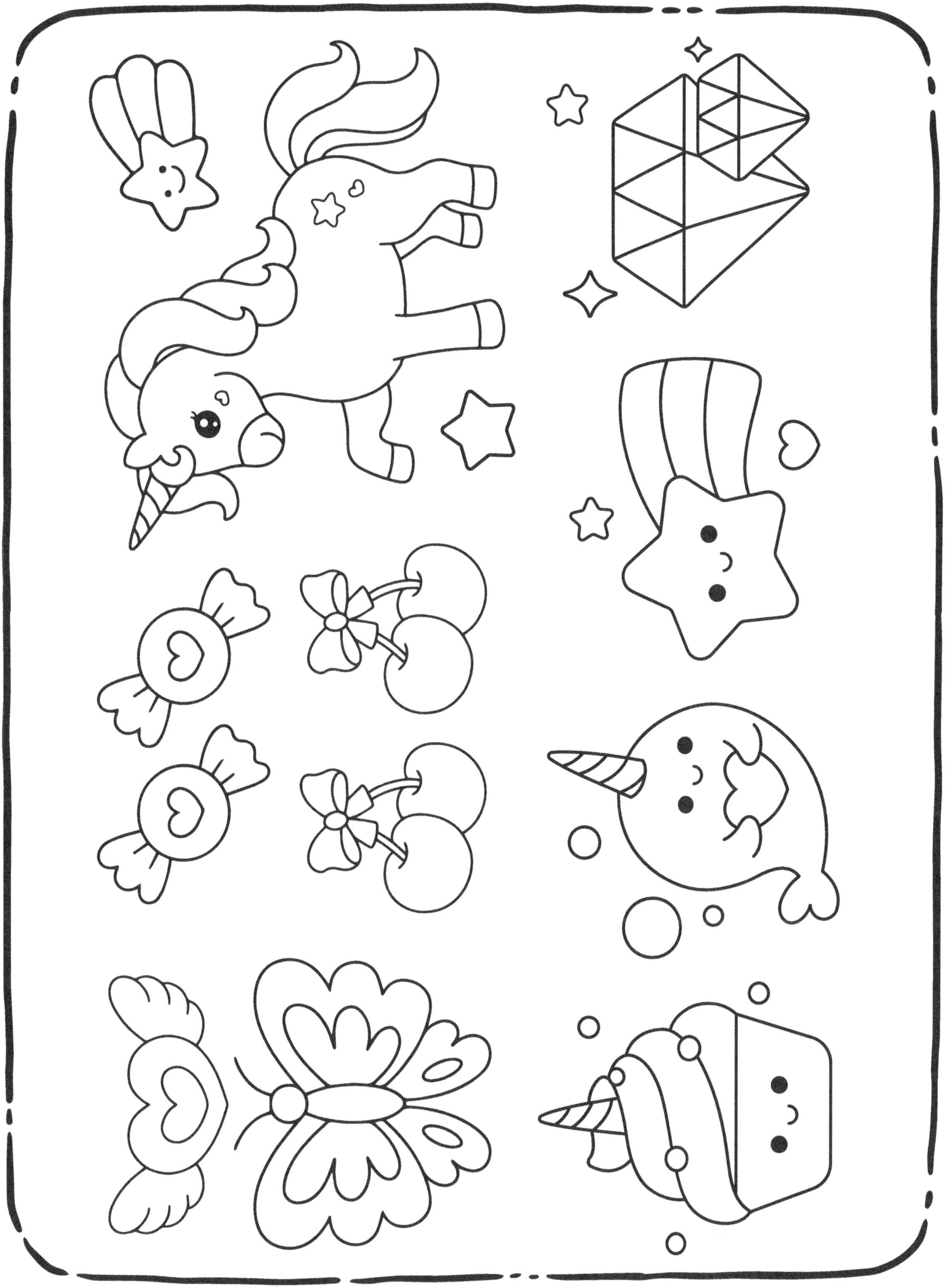

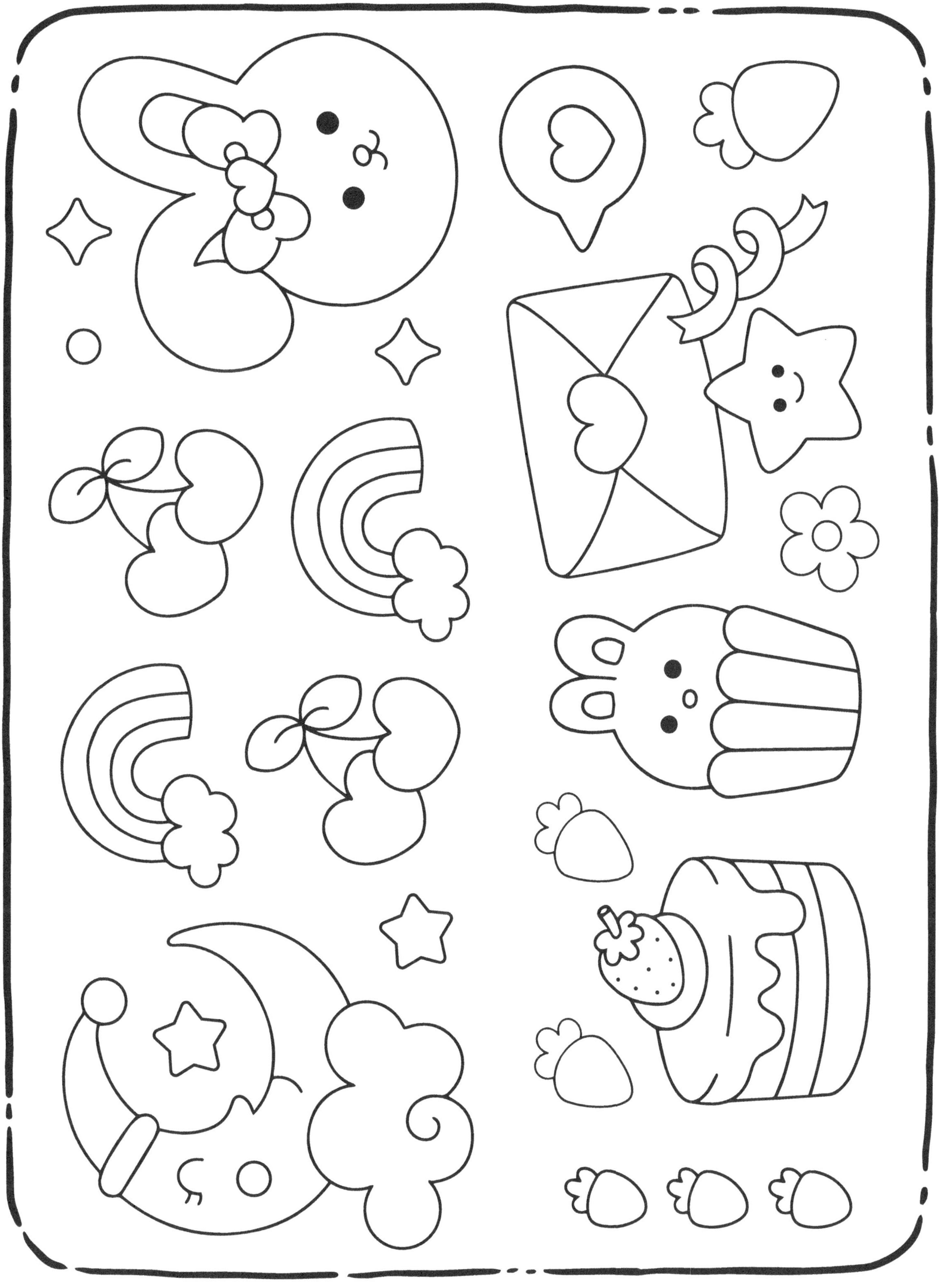

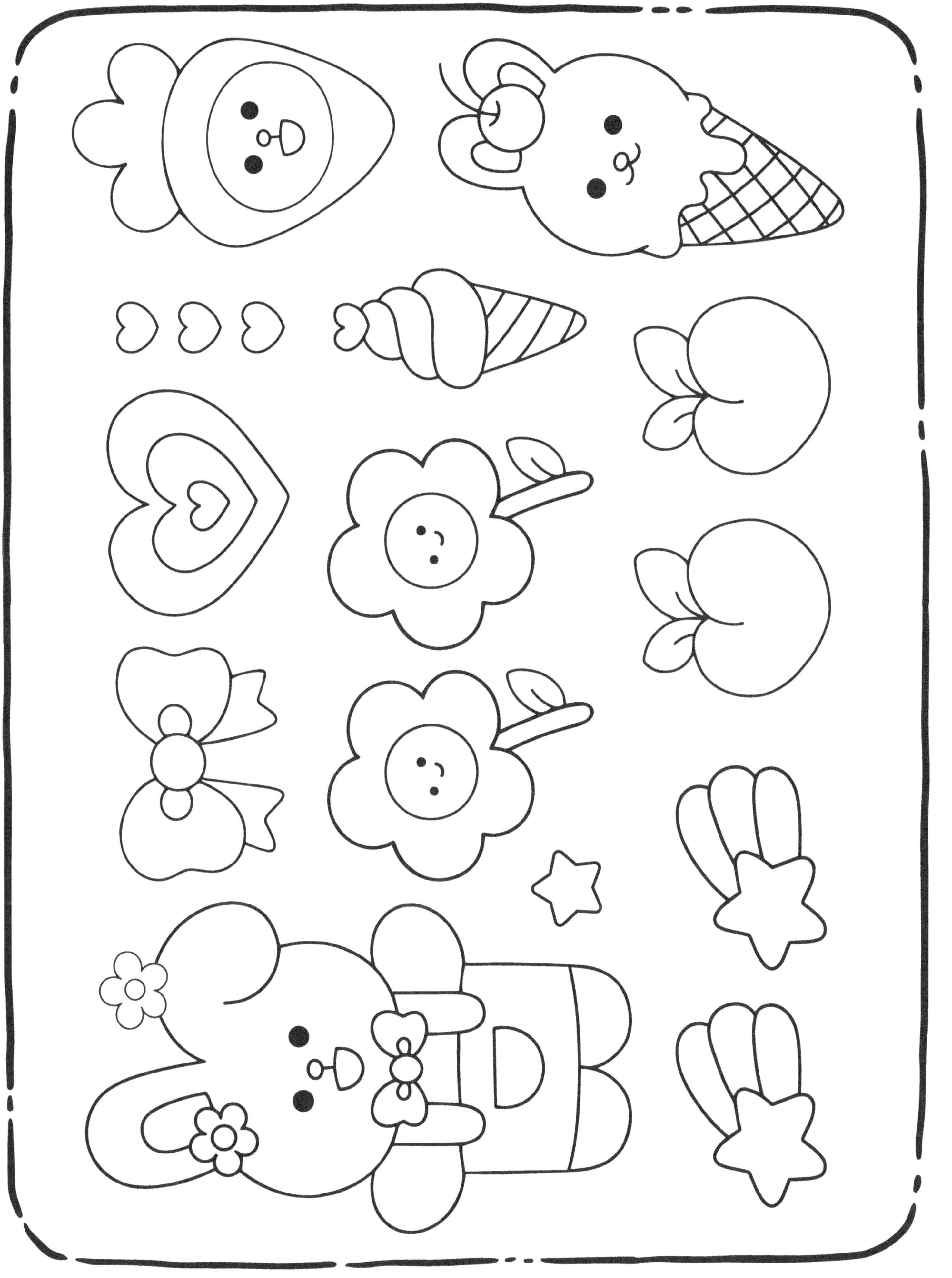

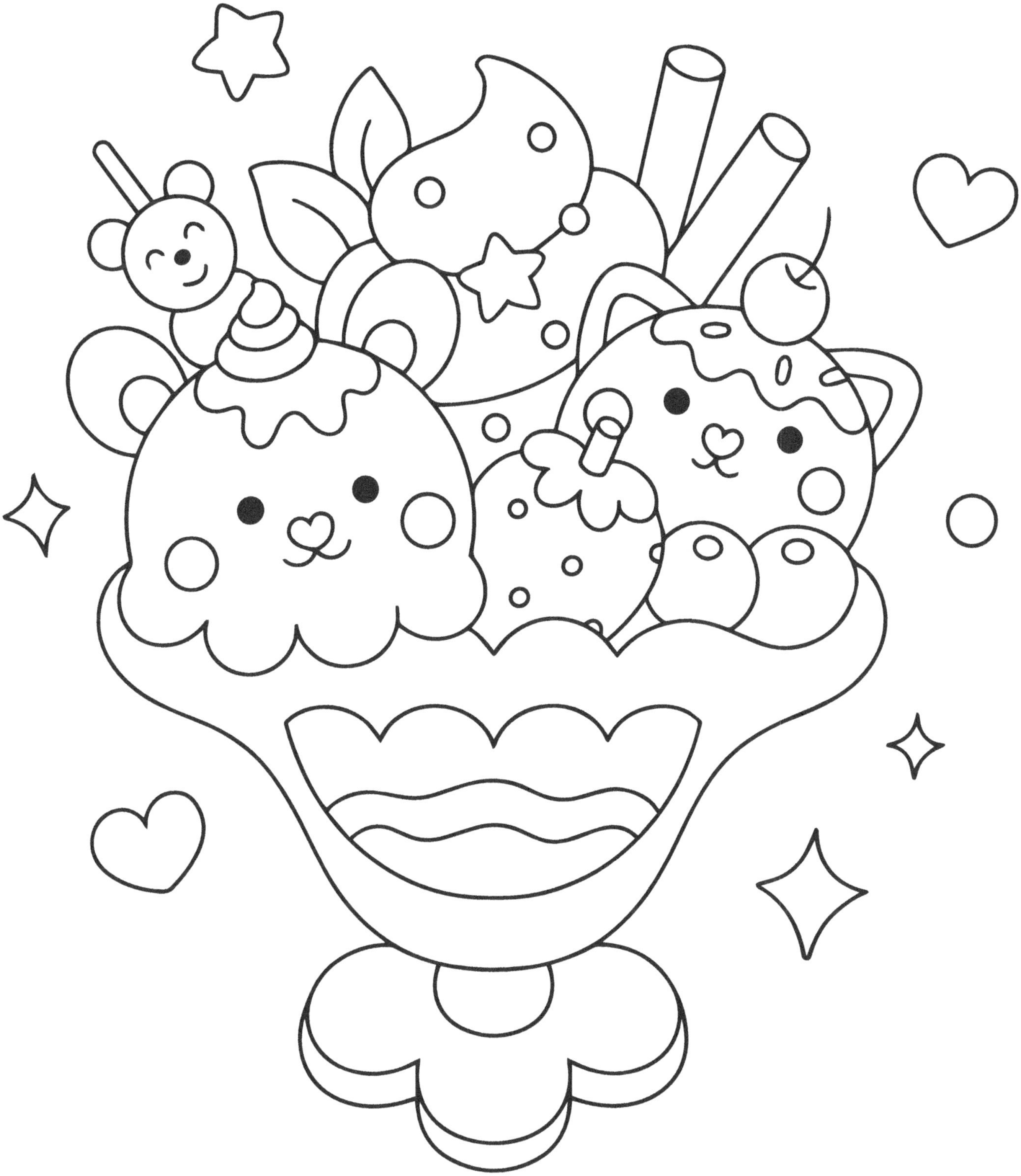

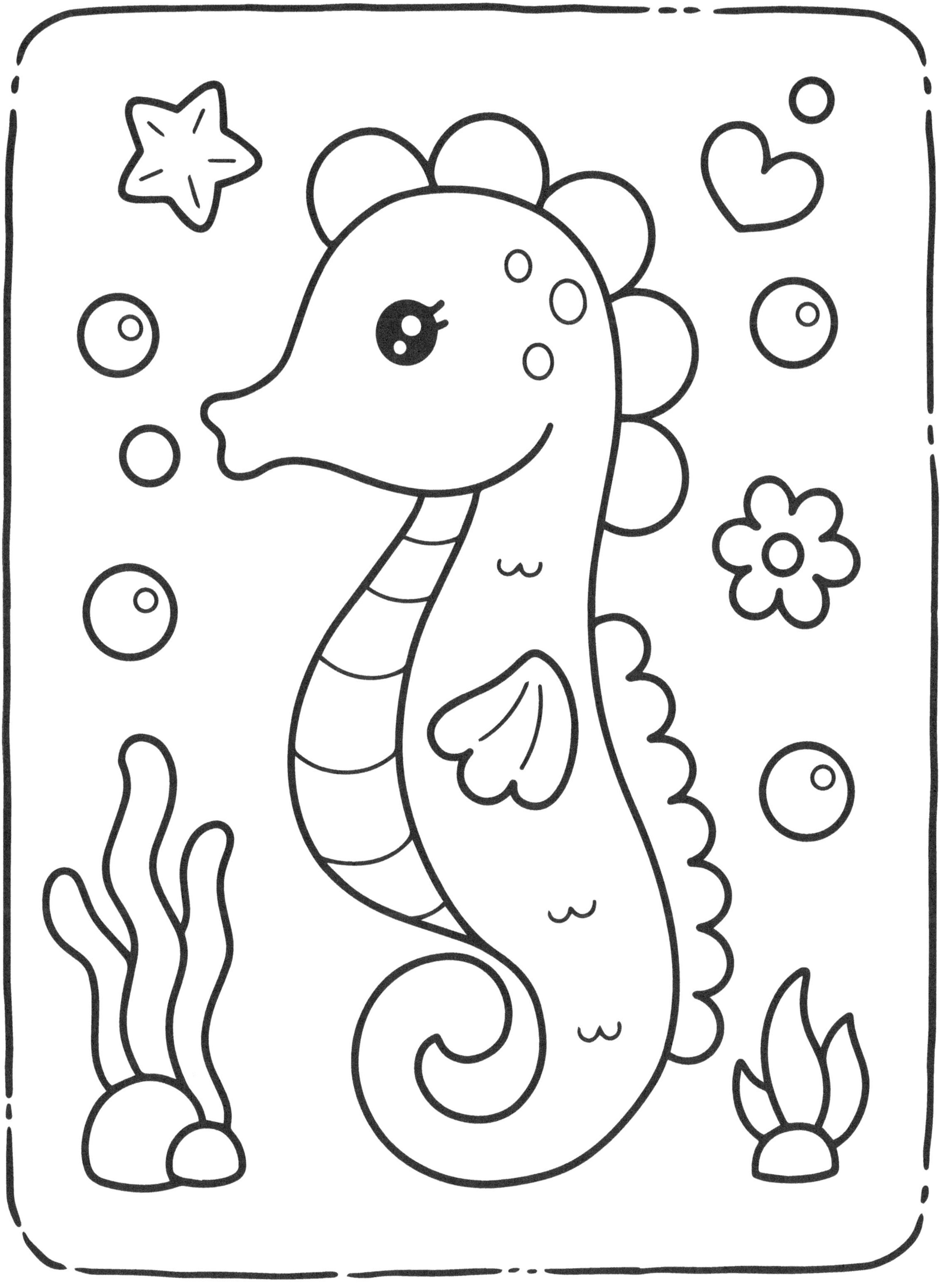

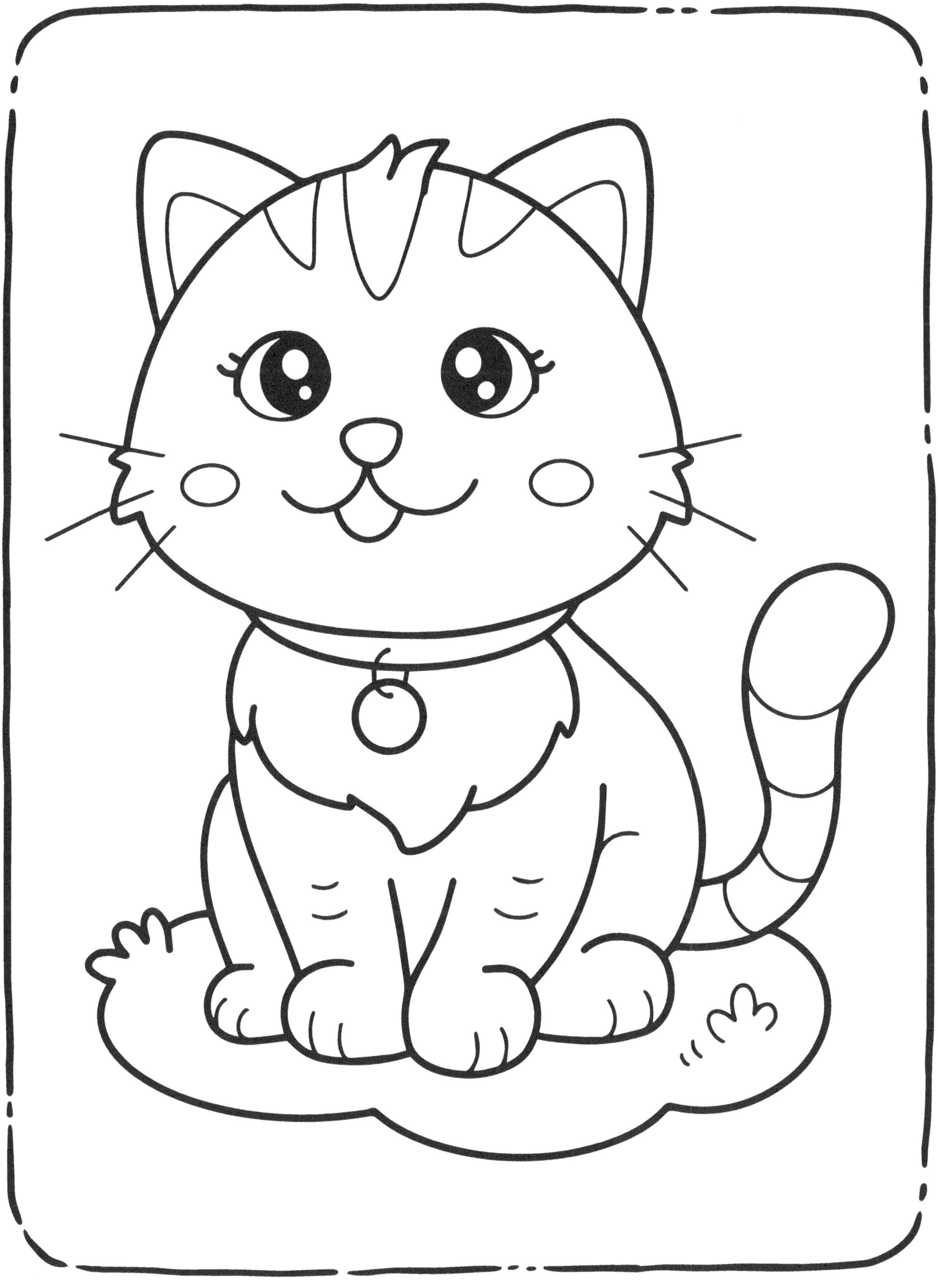

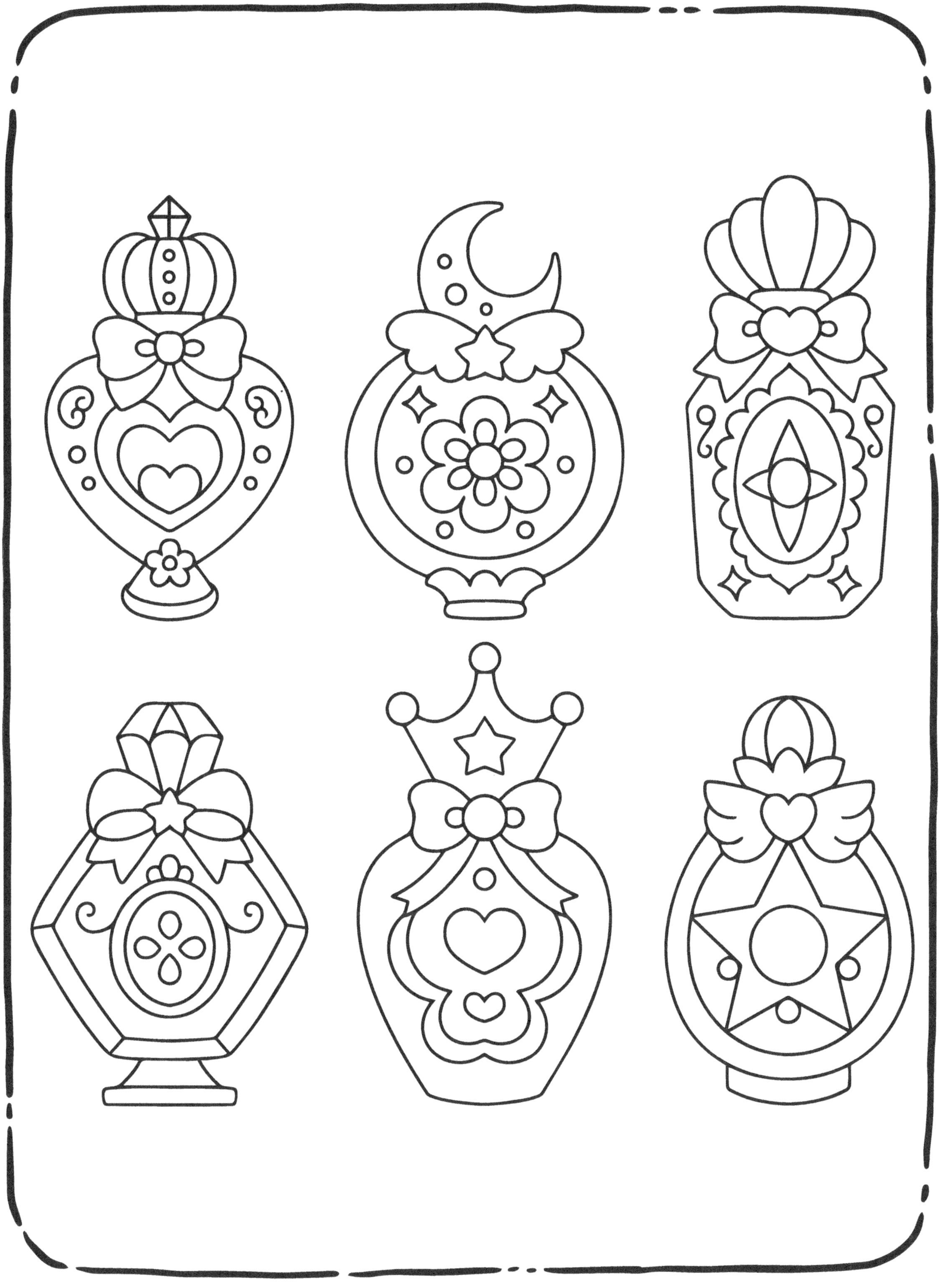

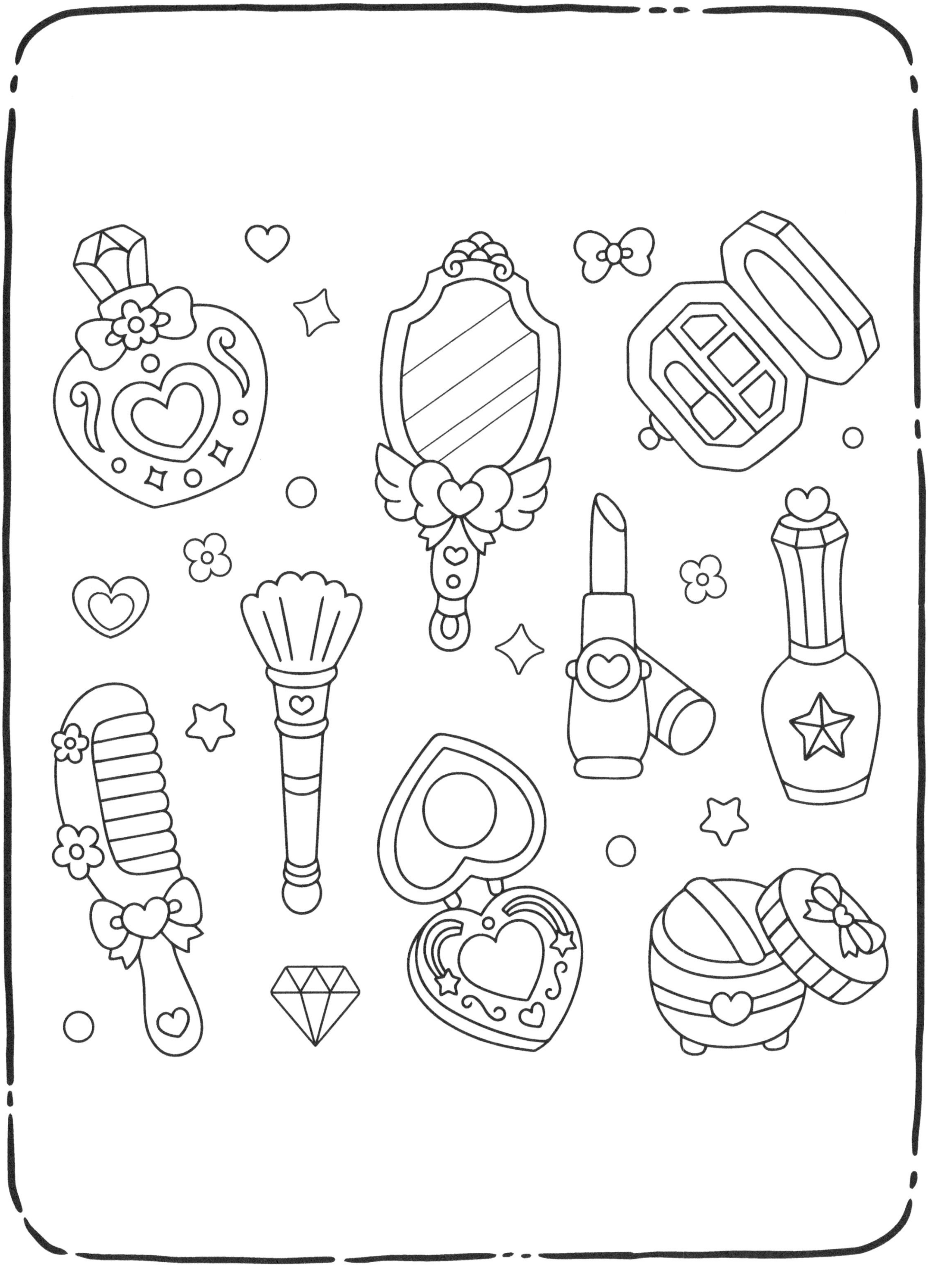

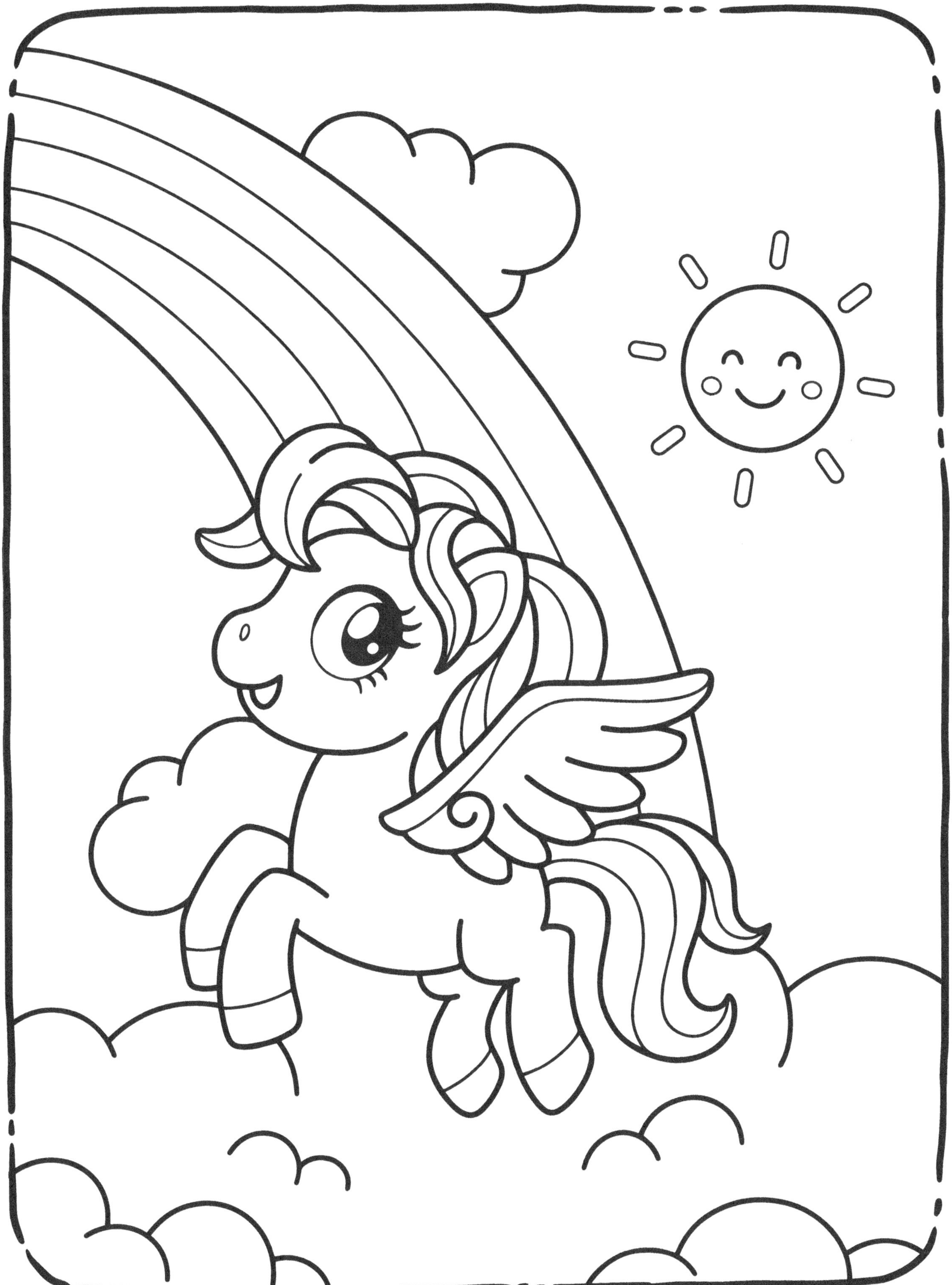

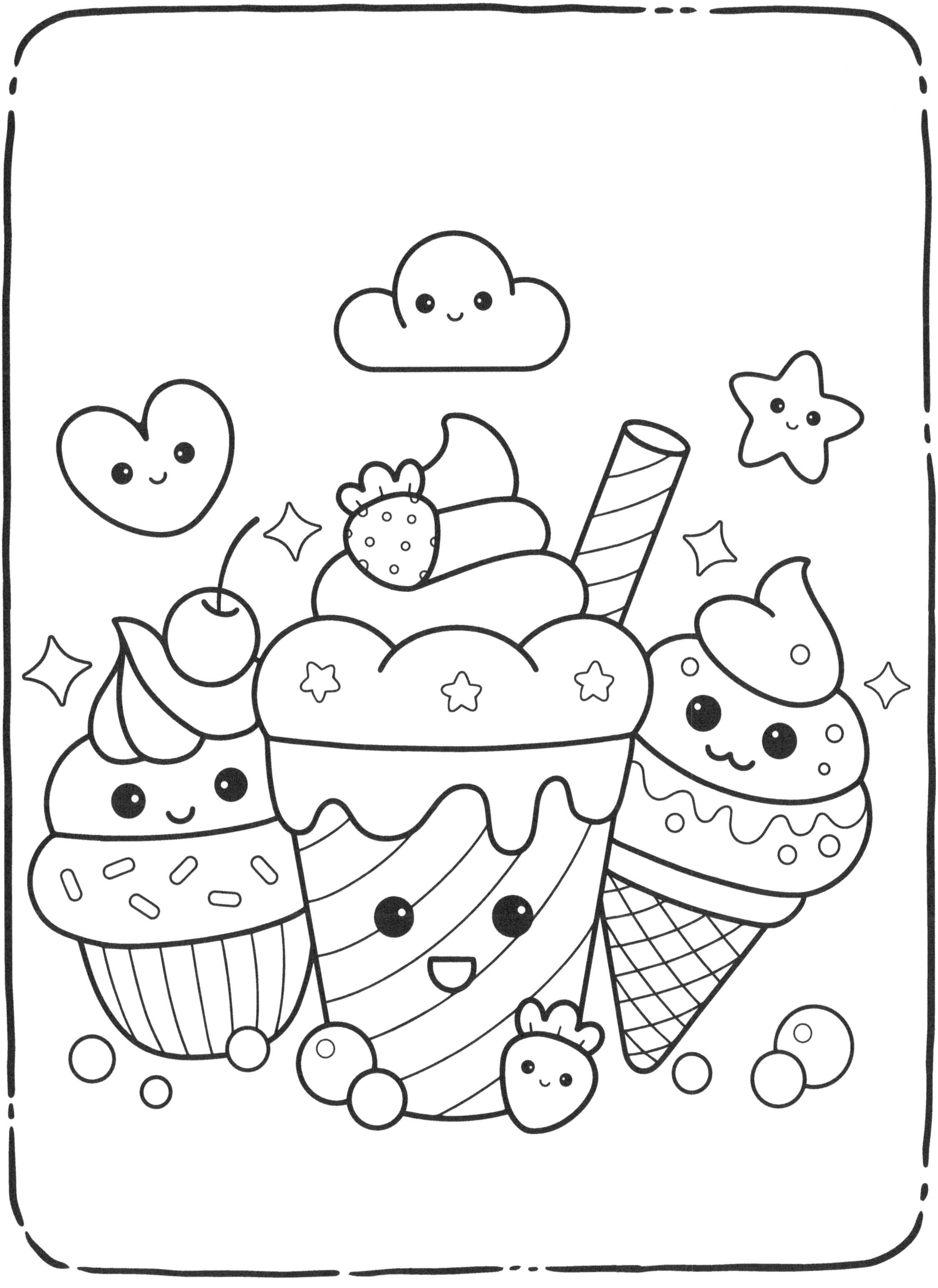

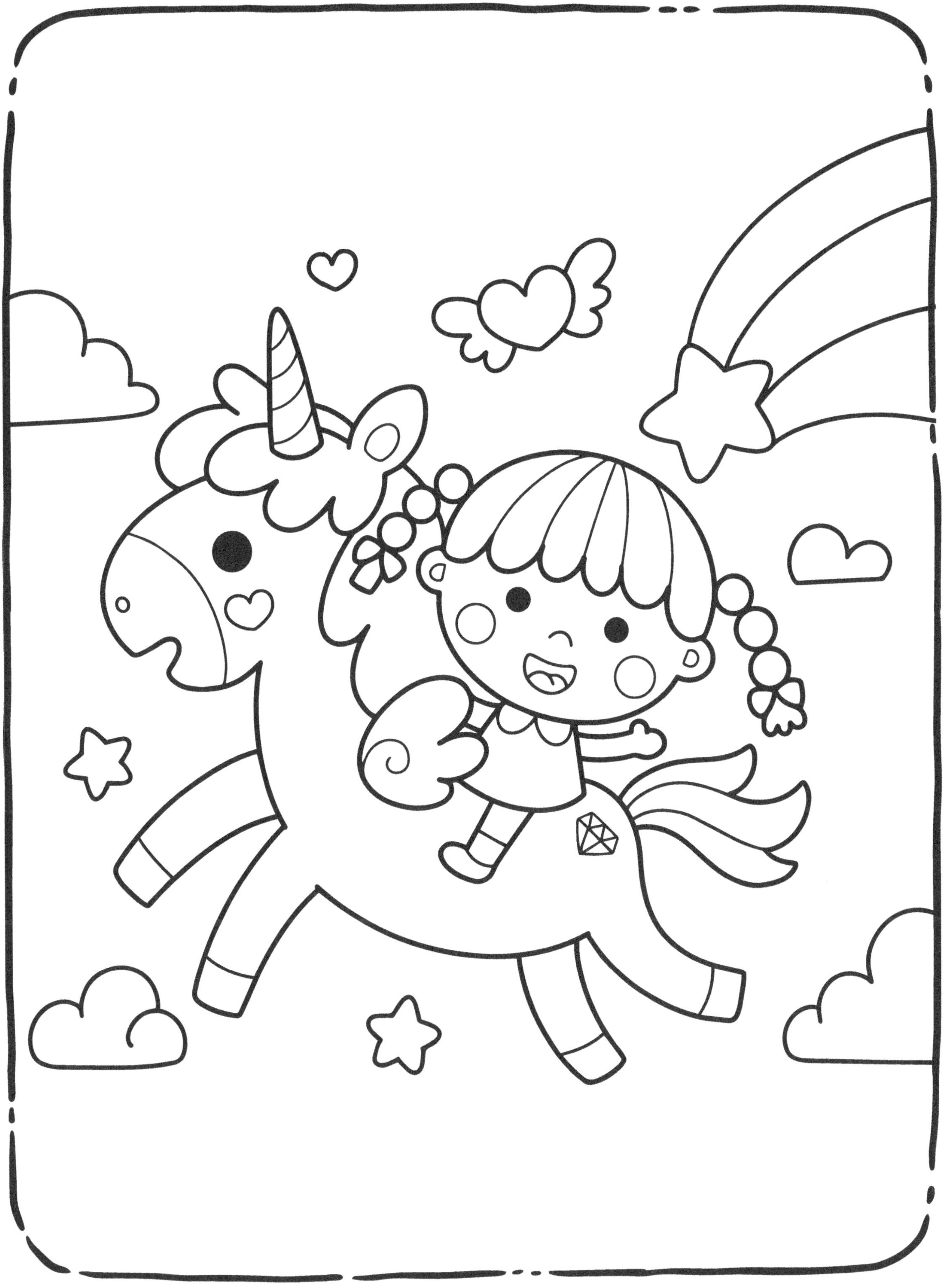

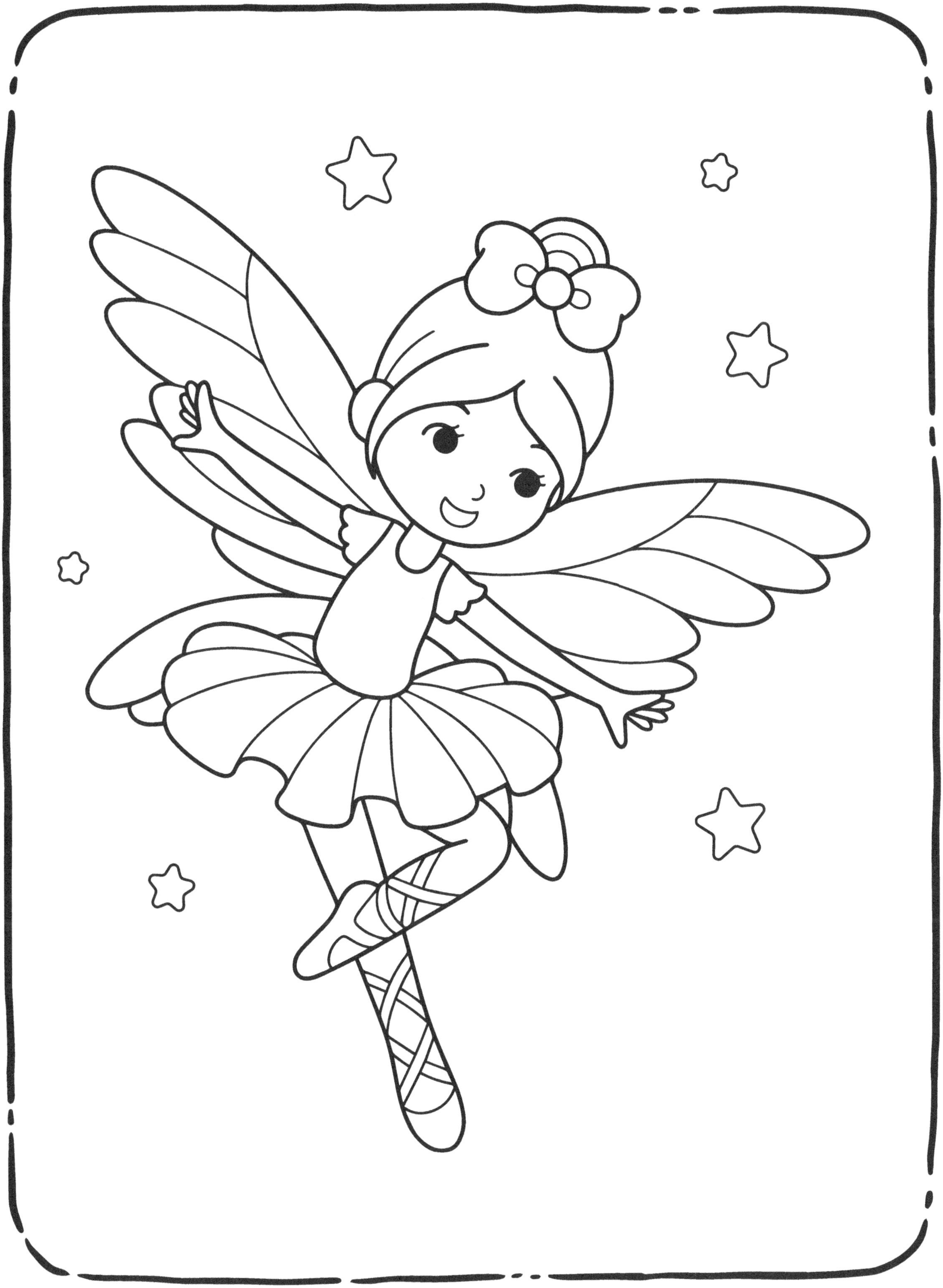

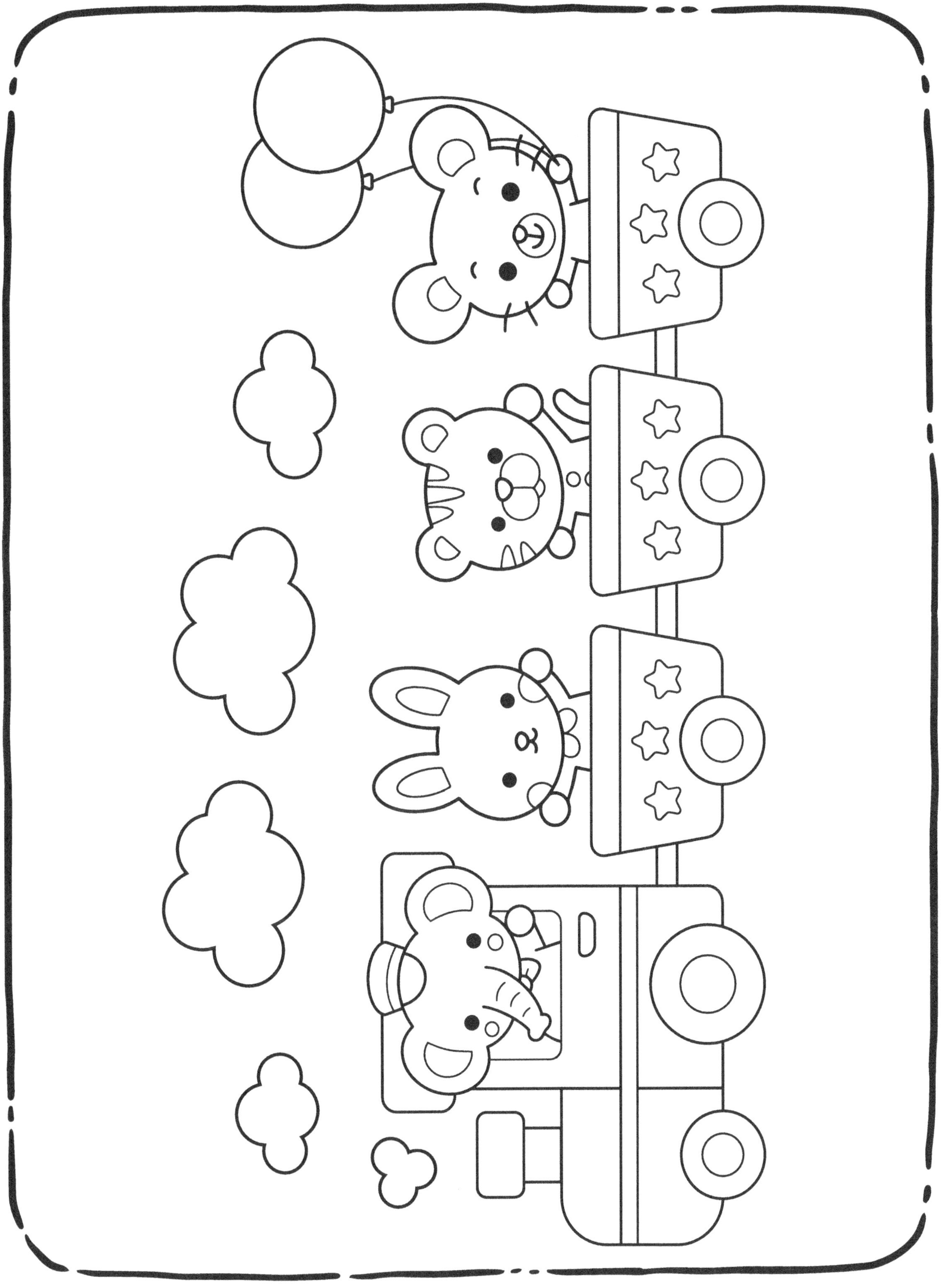

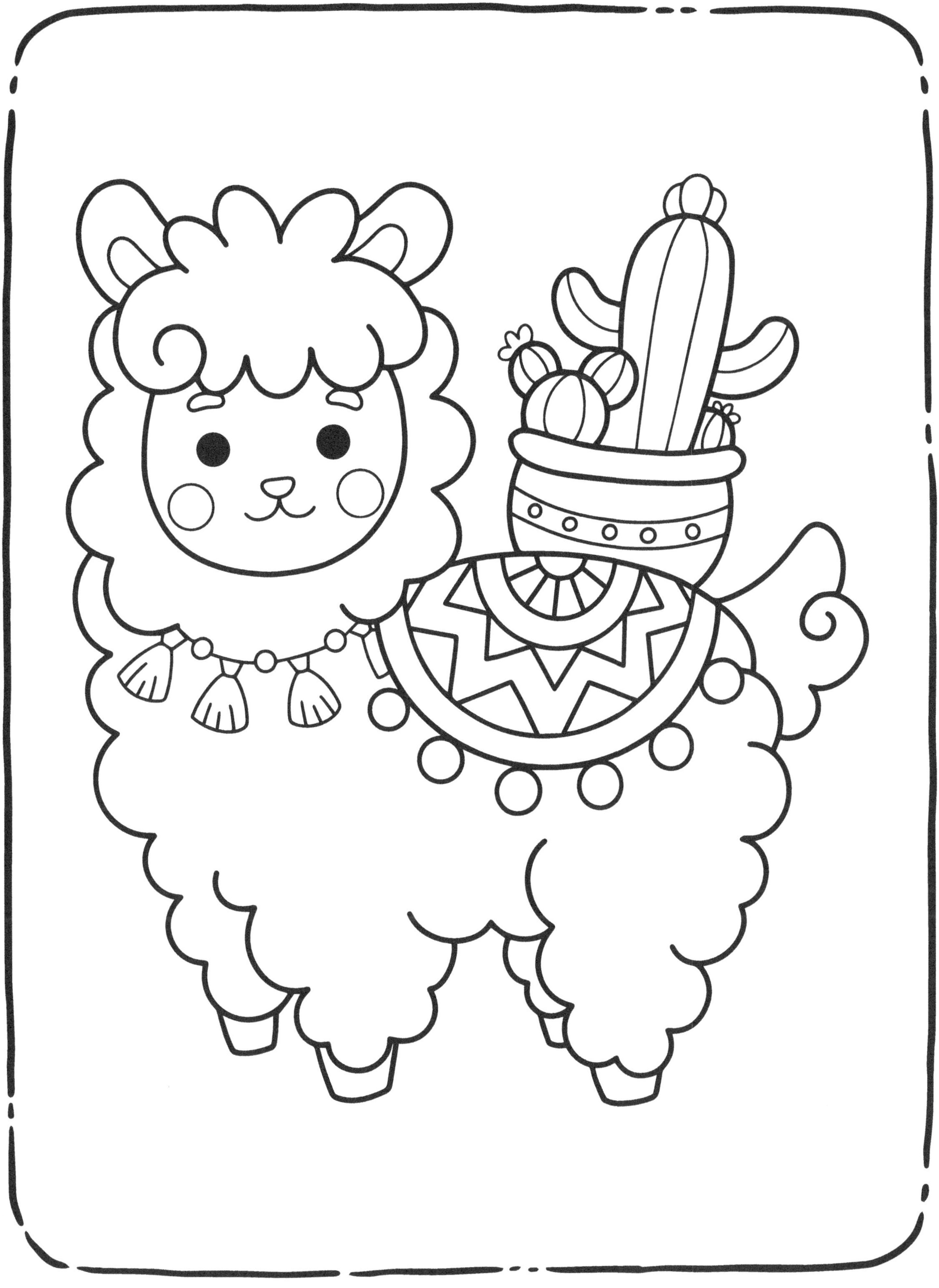

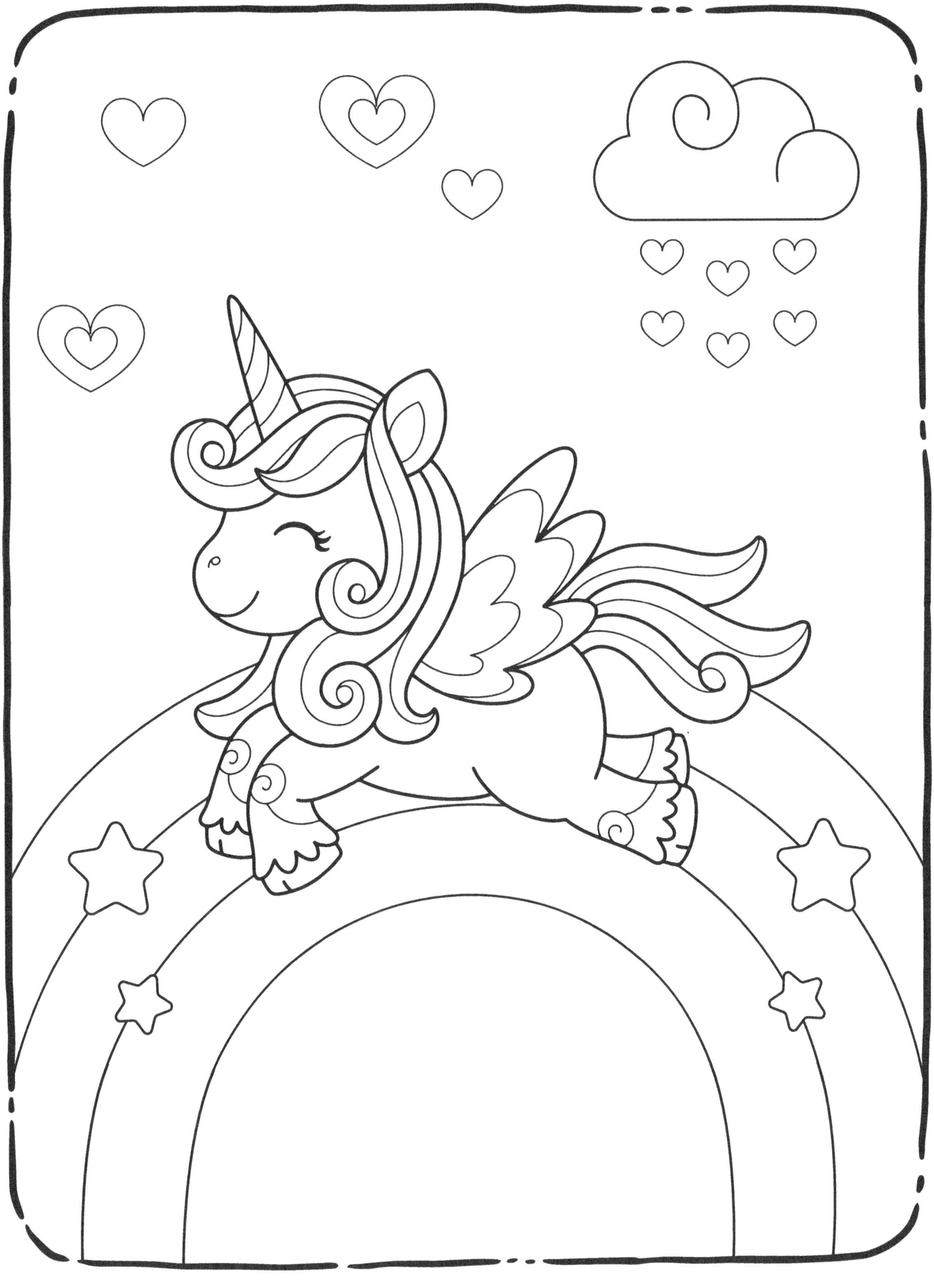

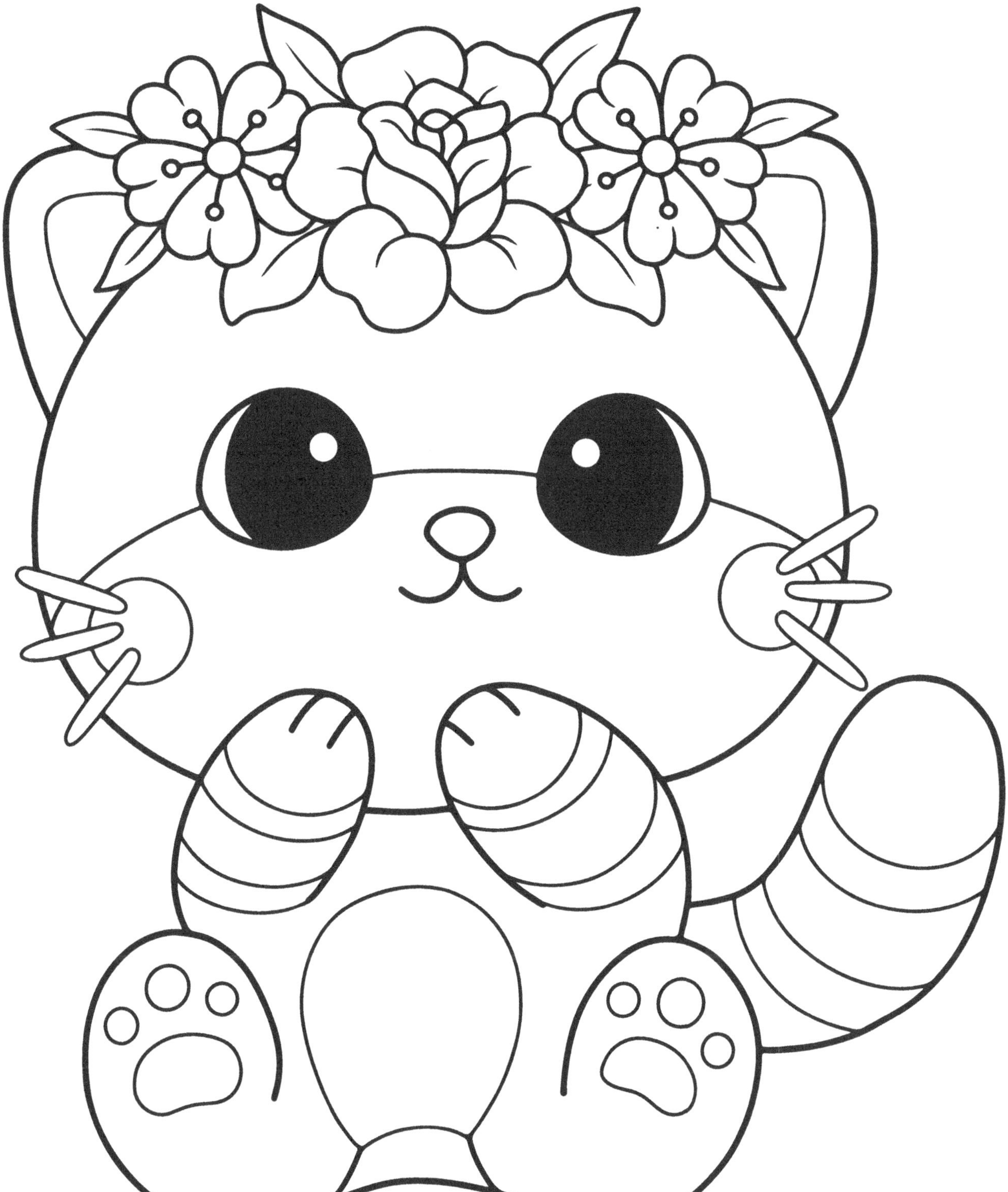

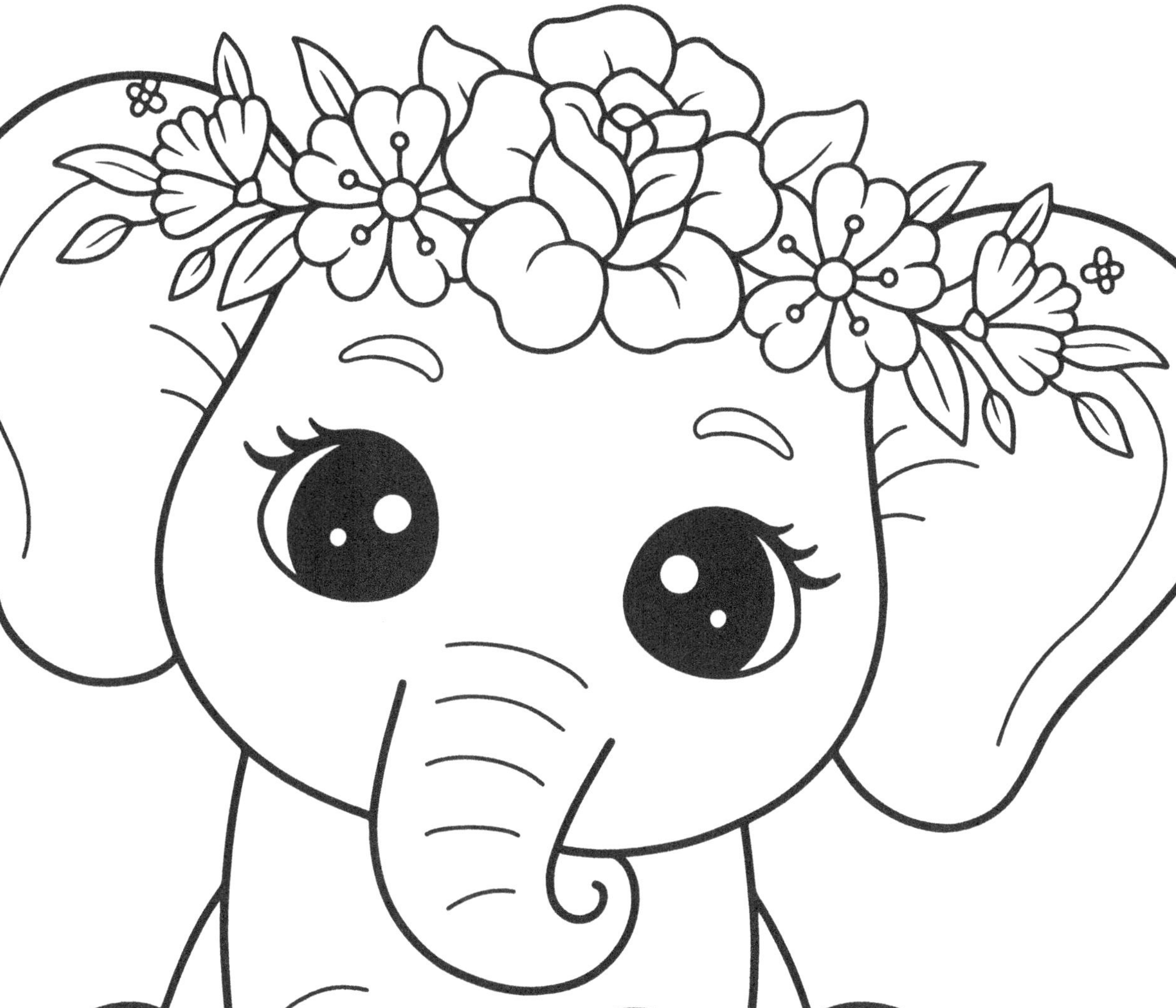

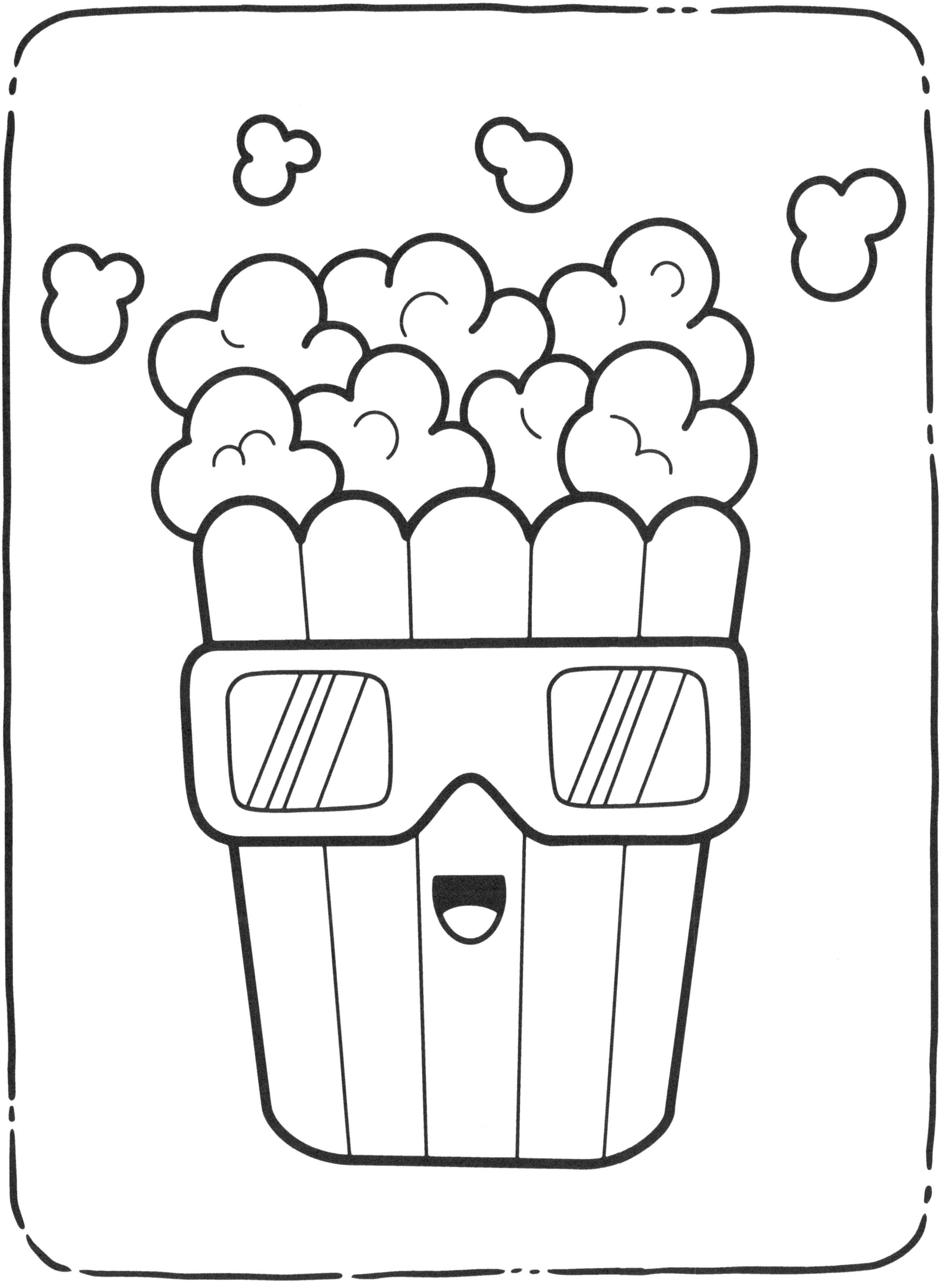

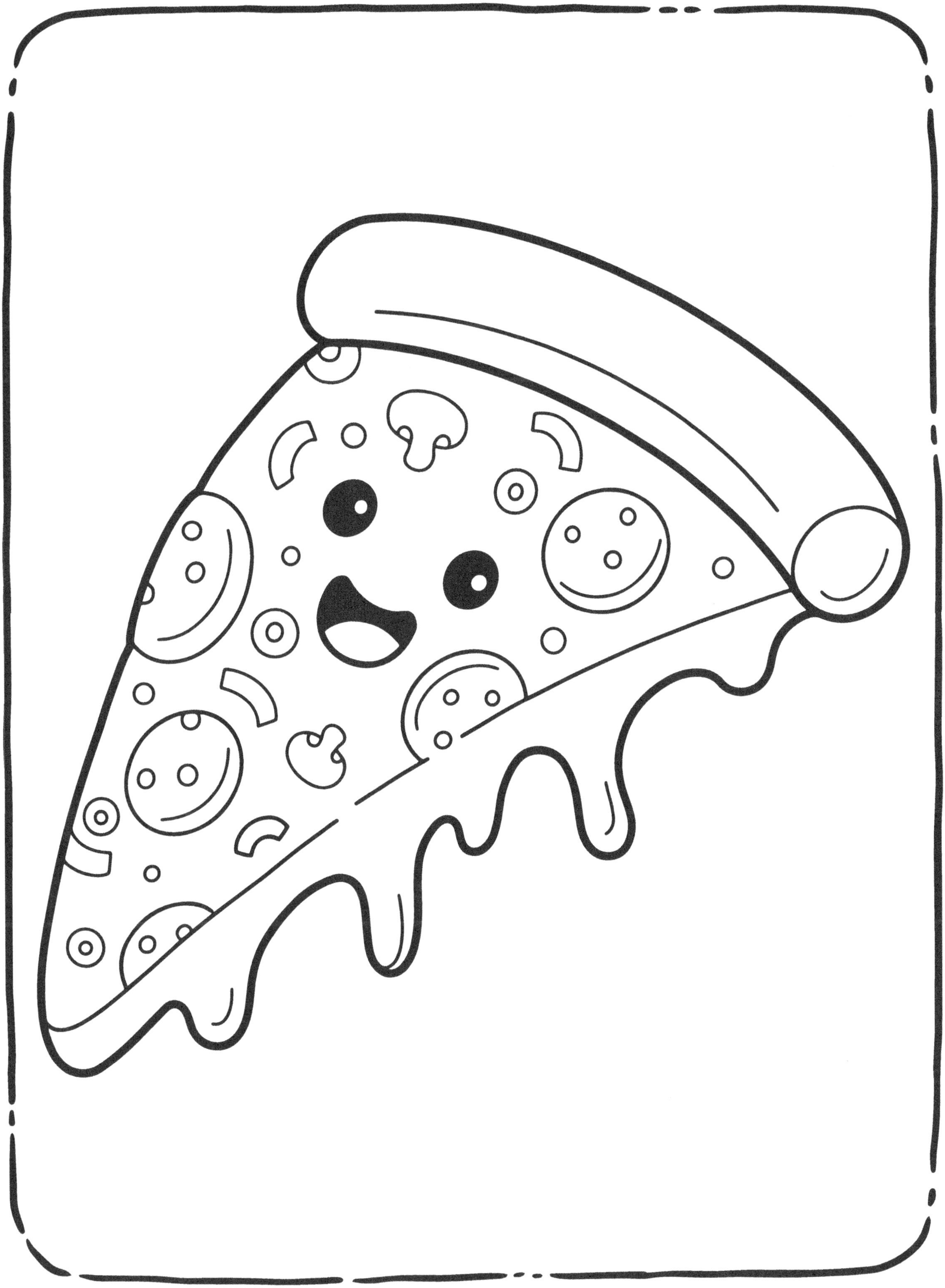

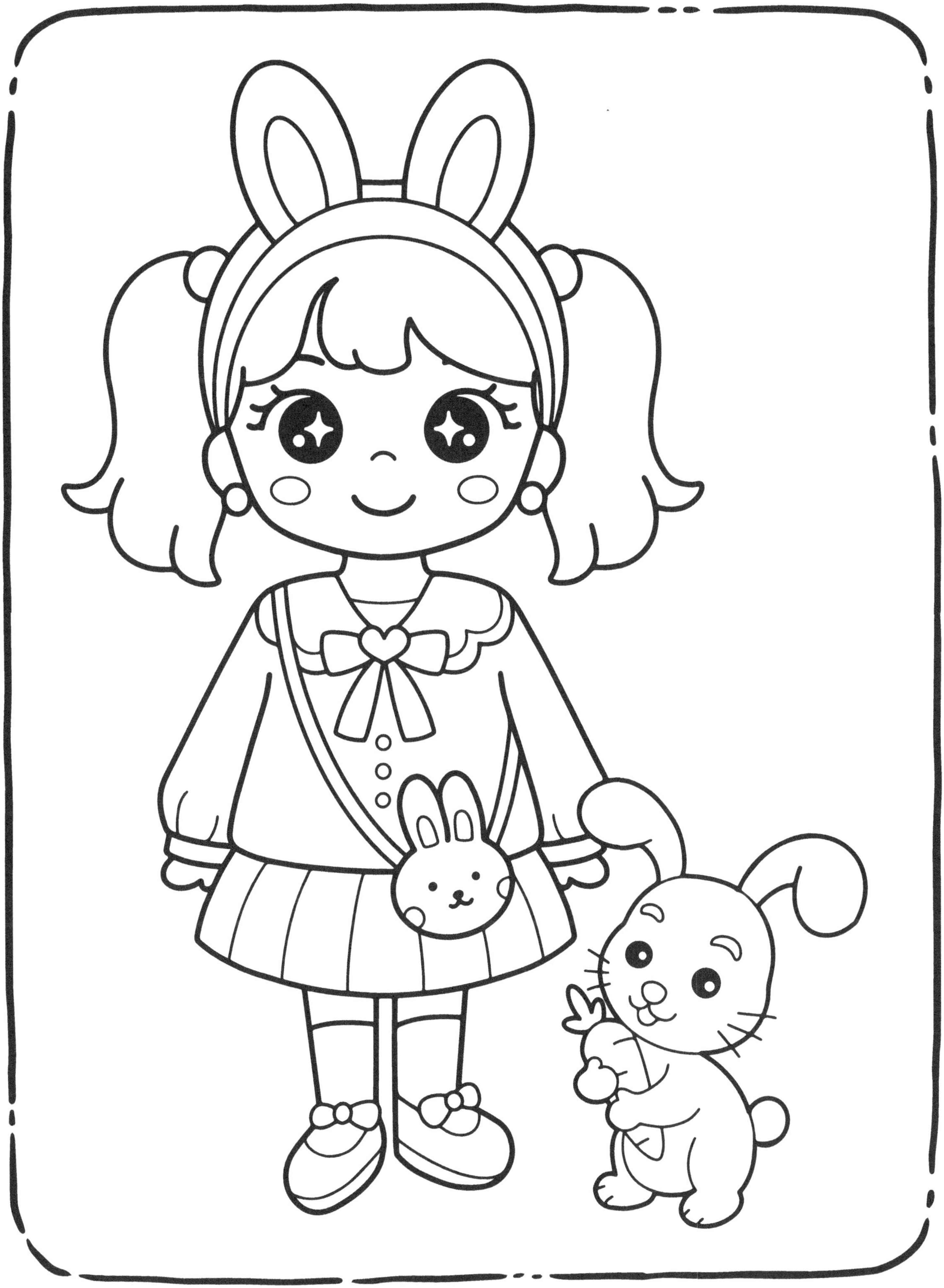

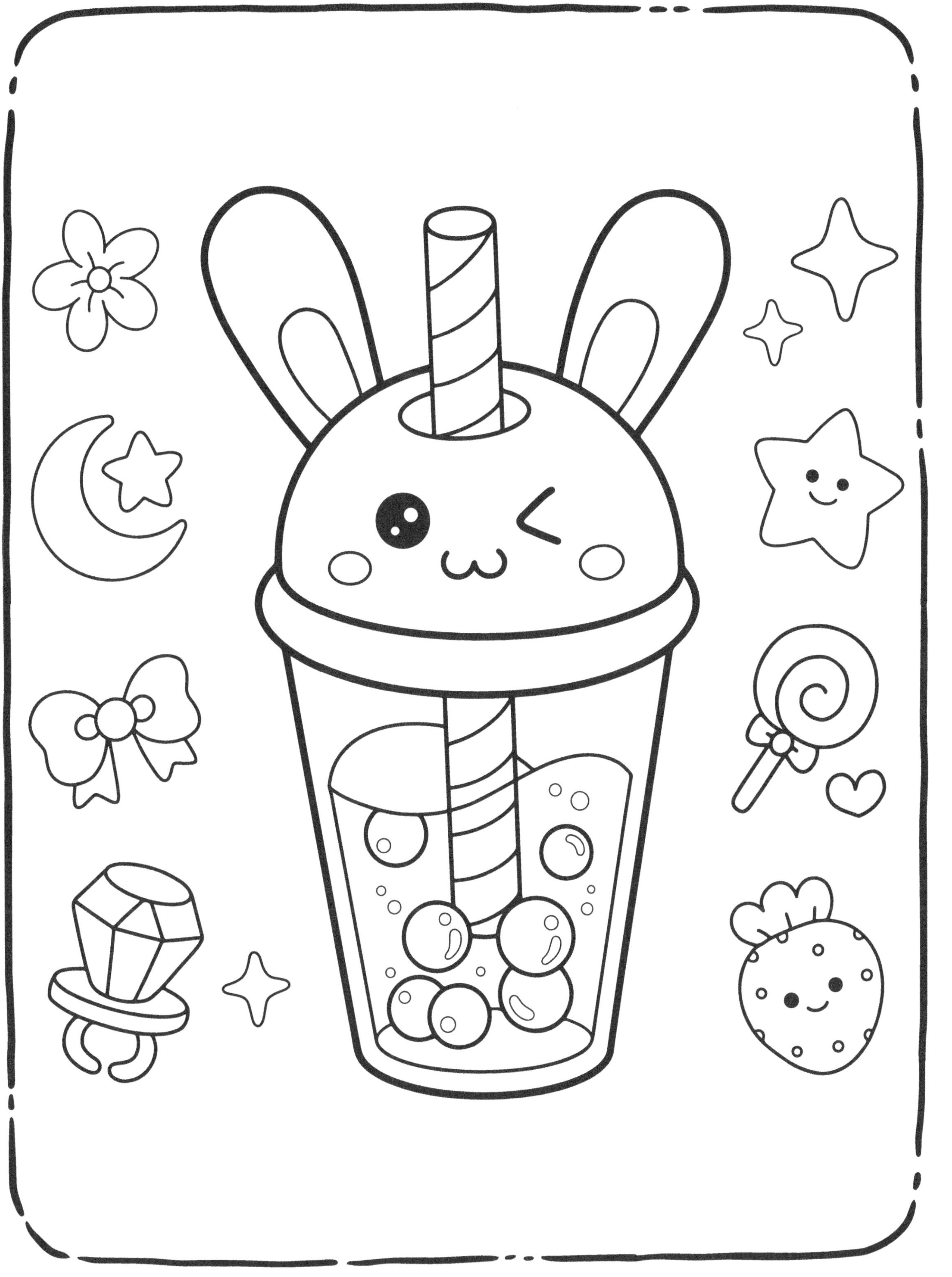

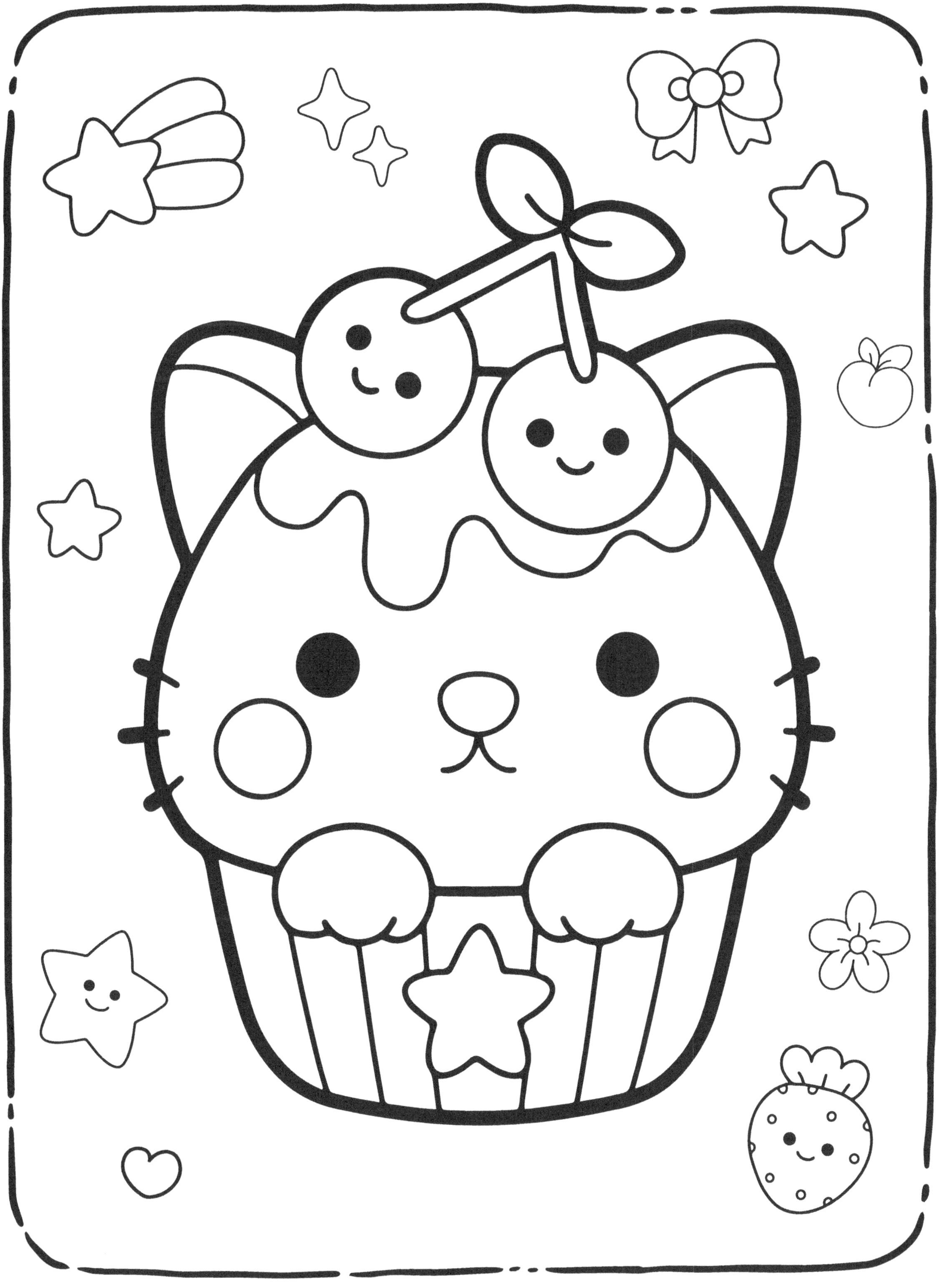

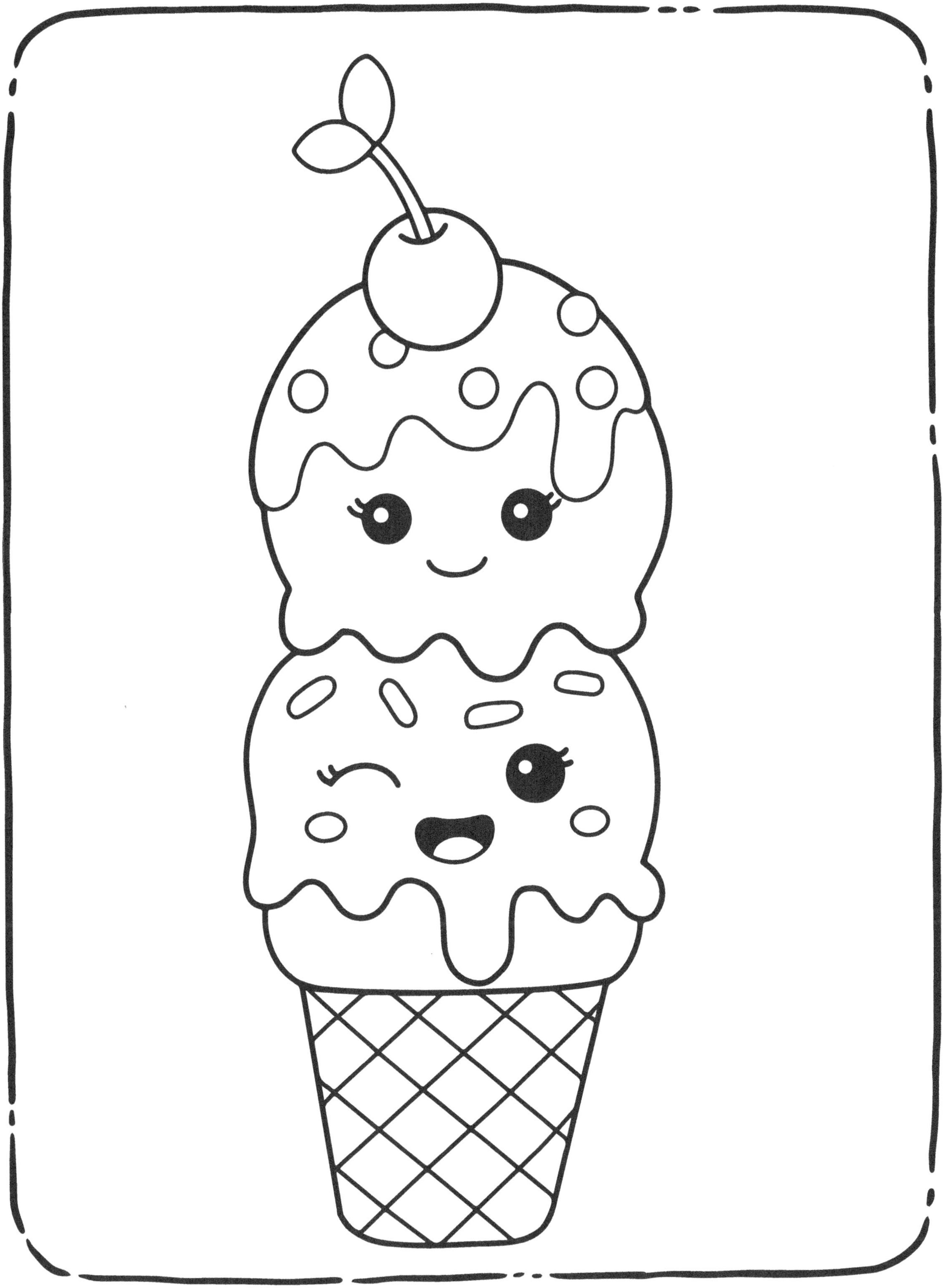

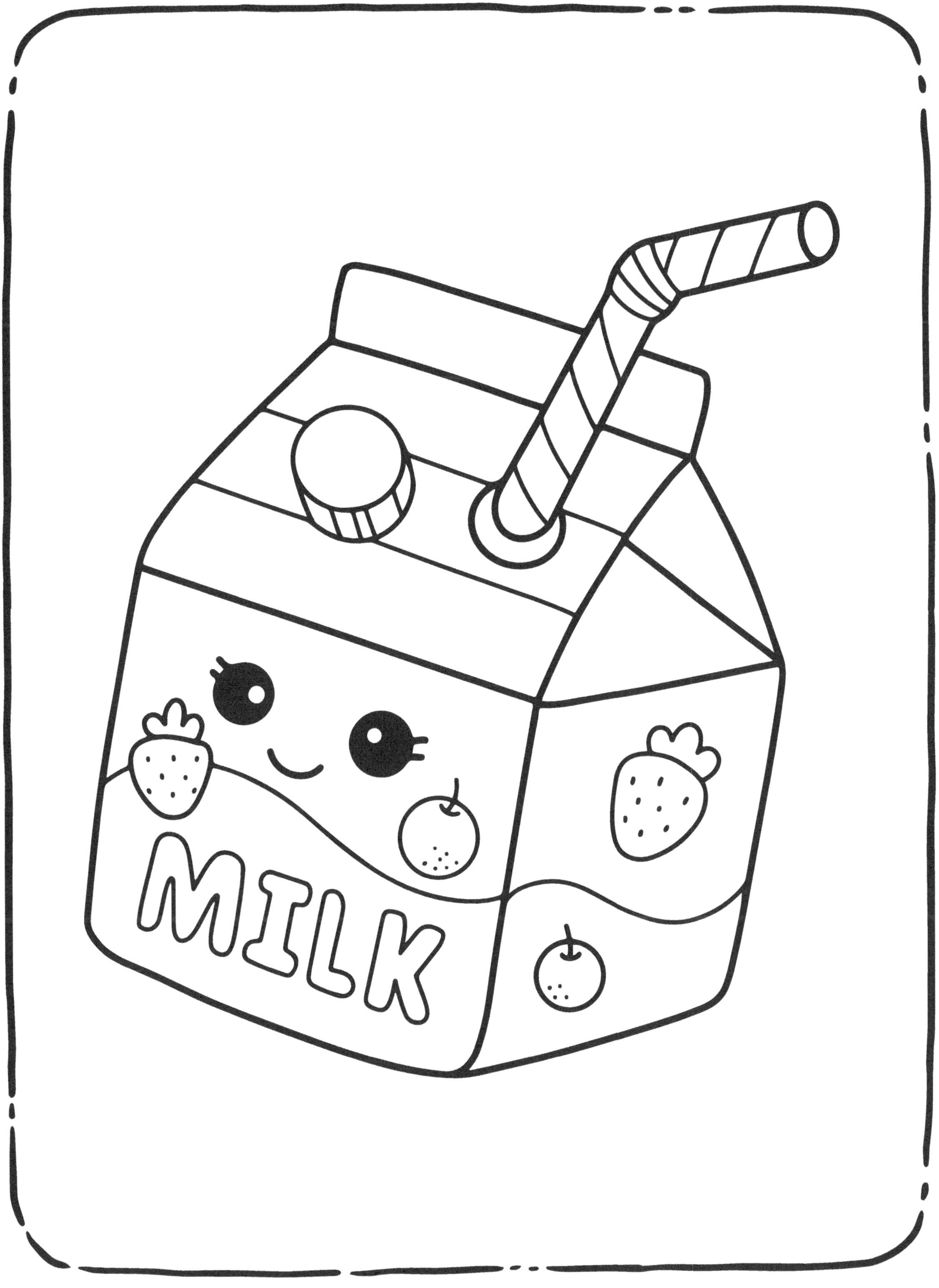
MILK

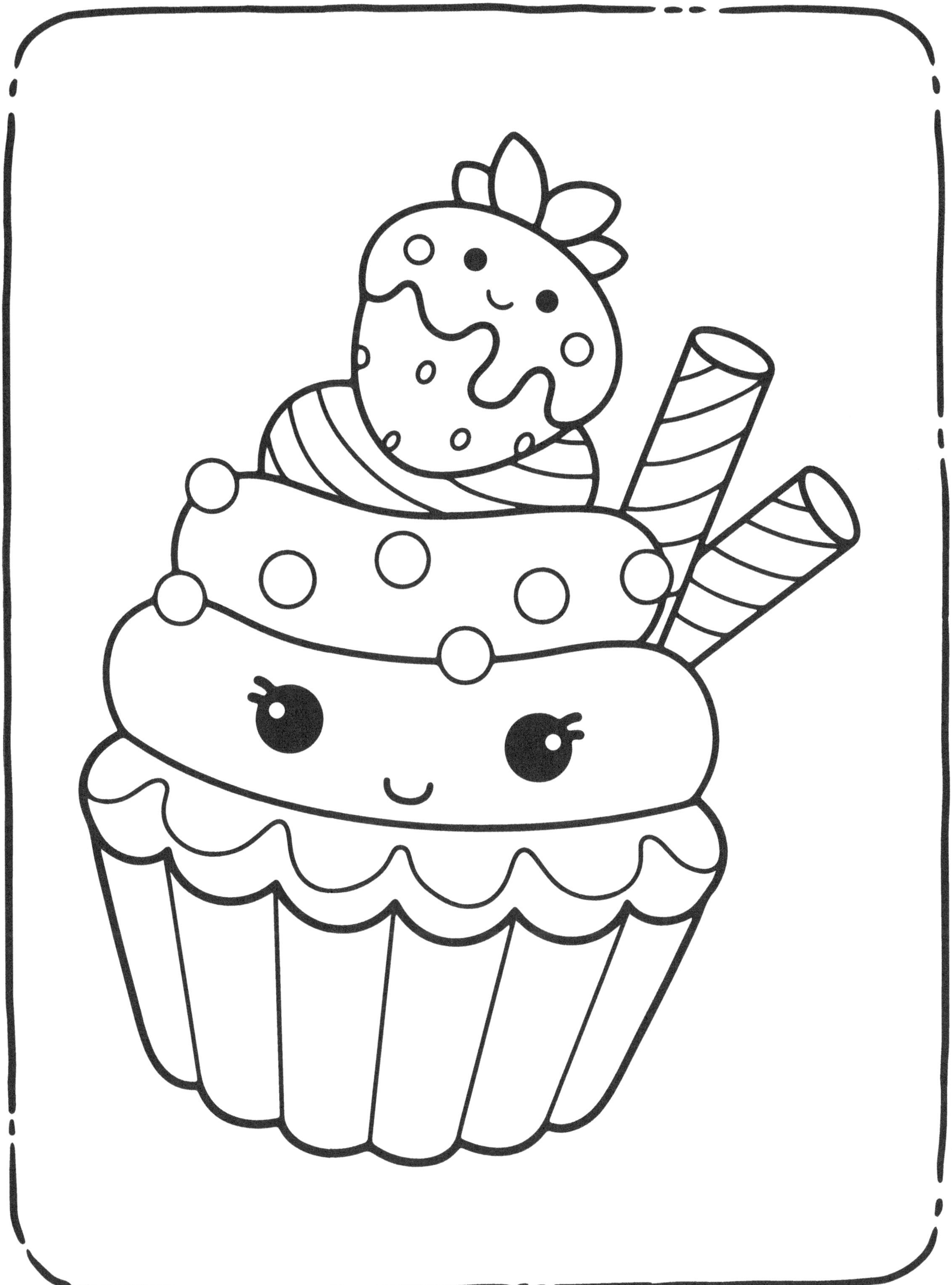

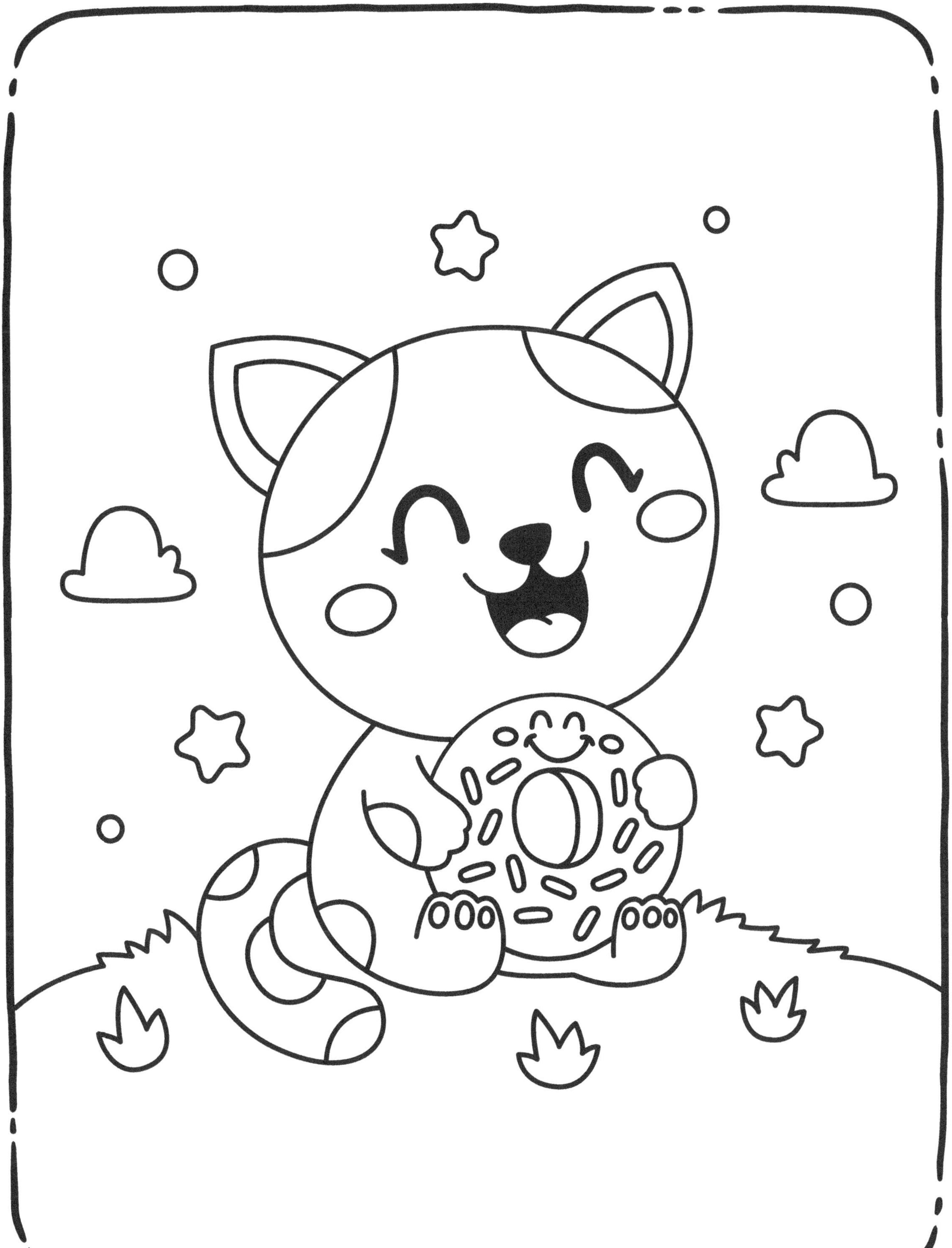

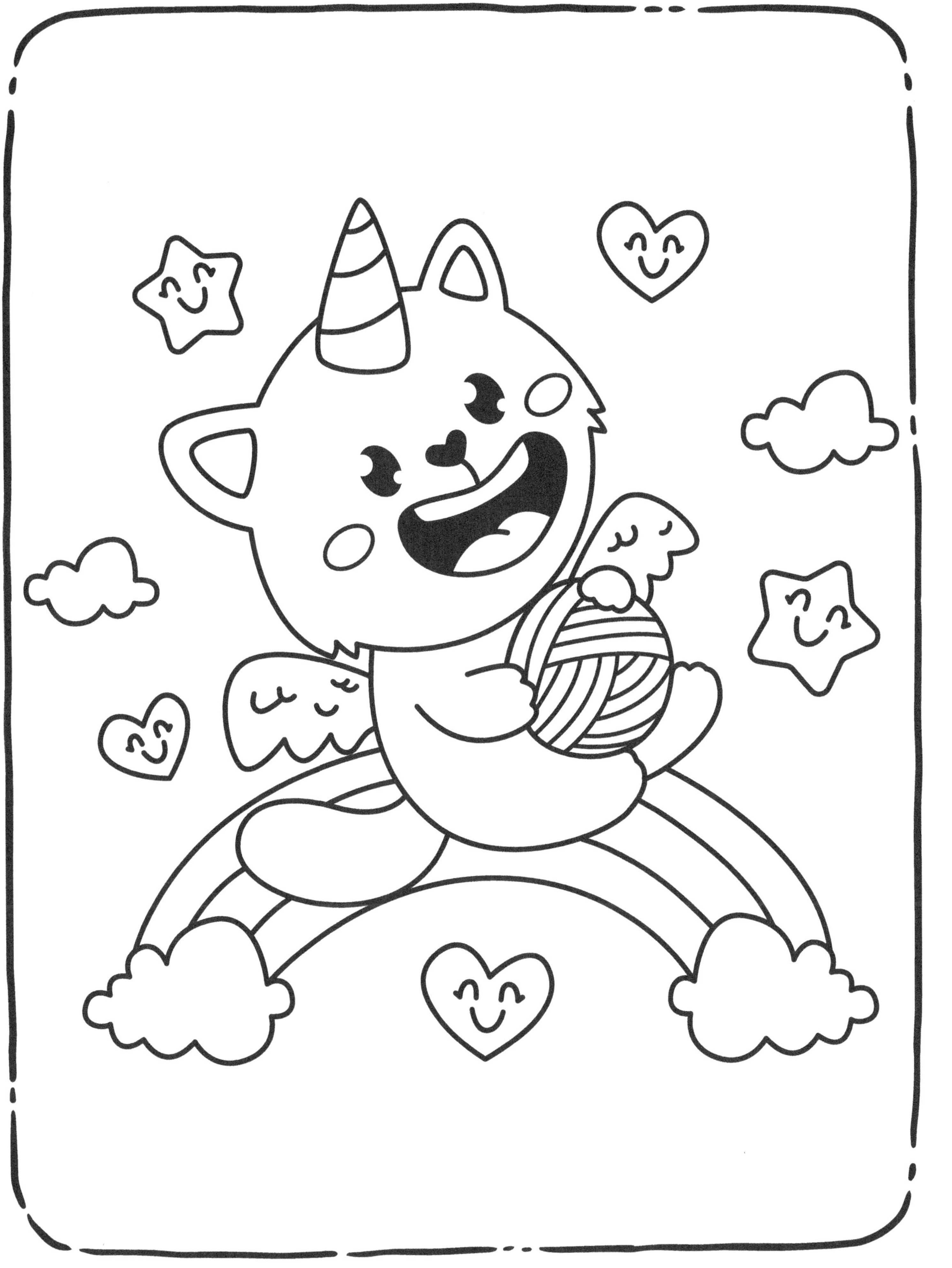

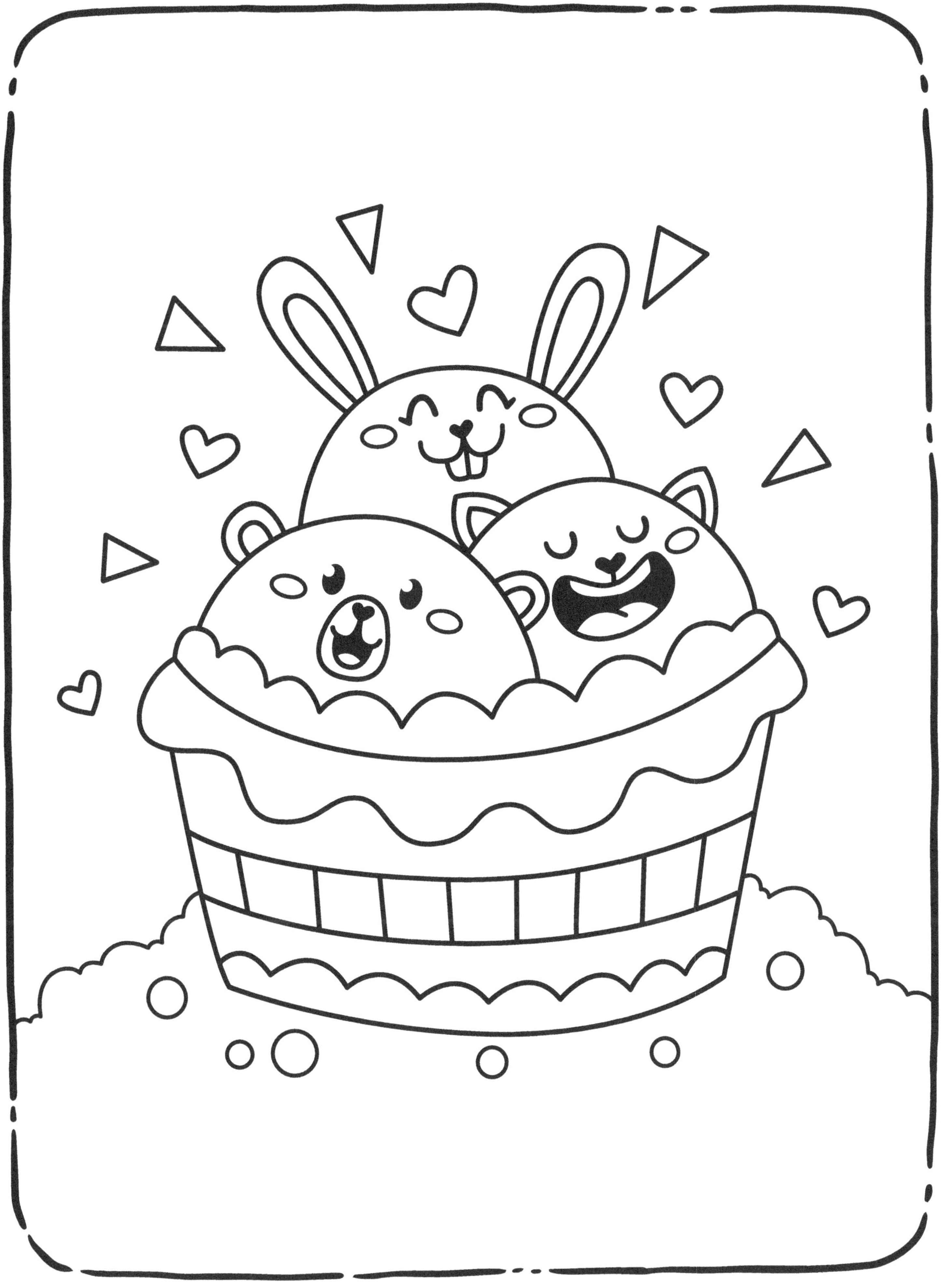

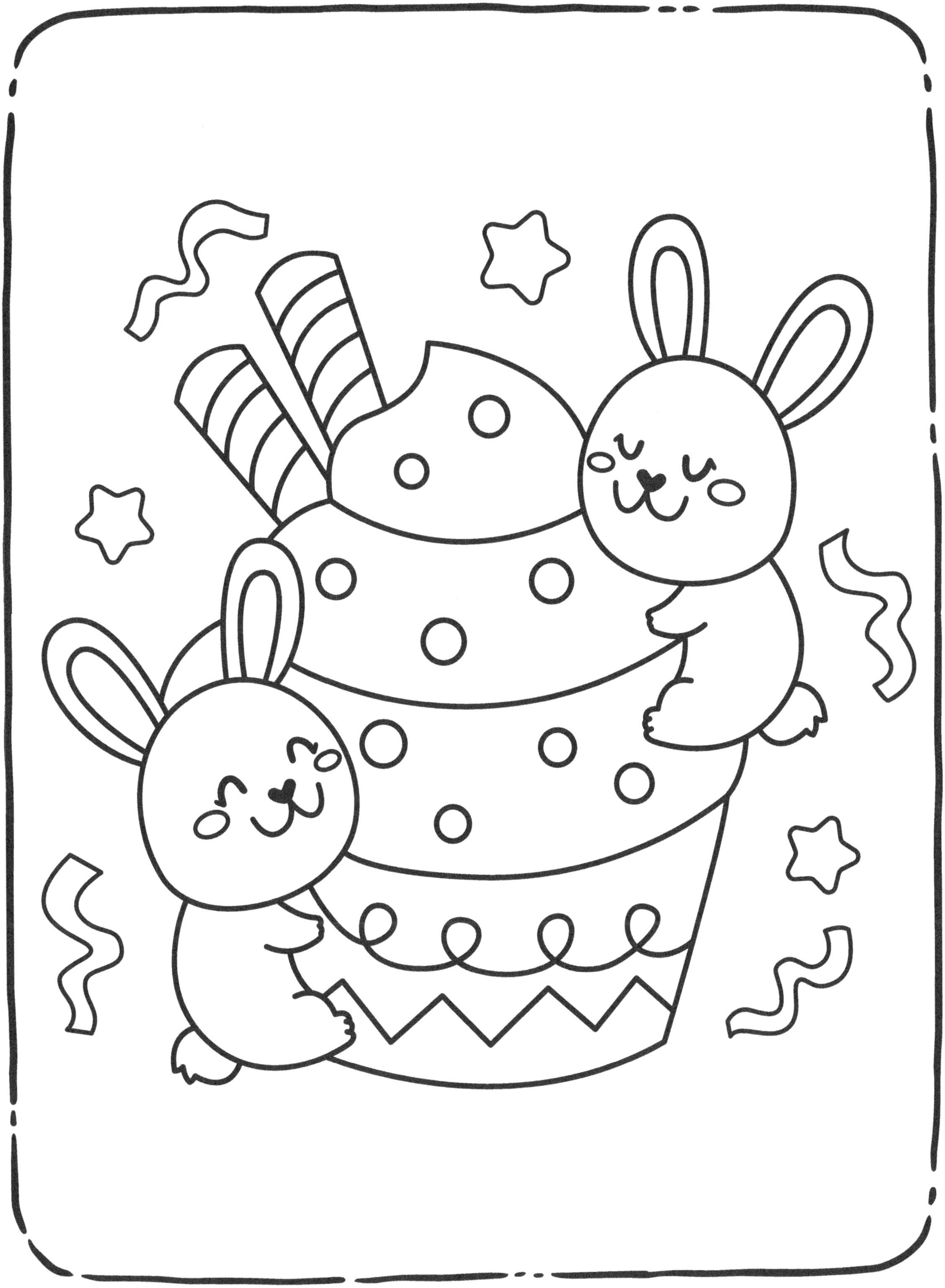

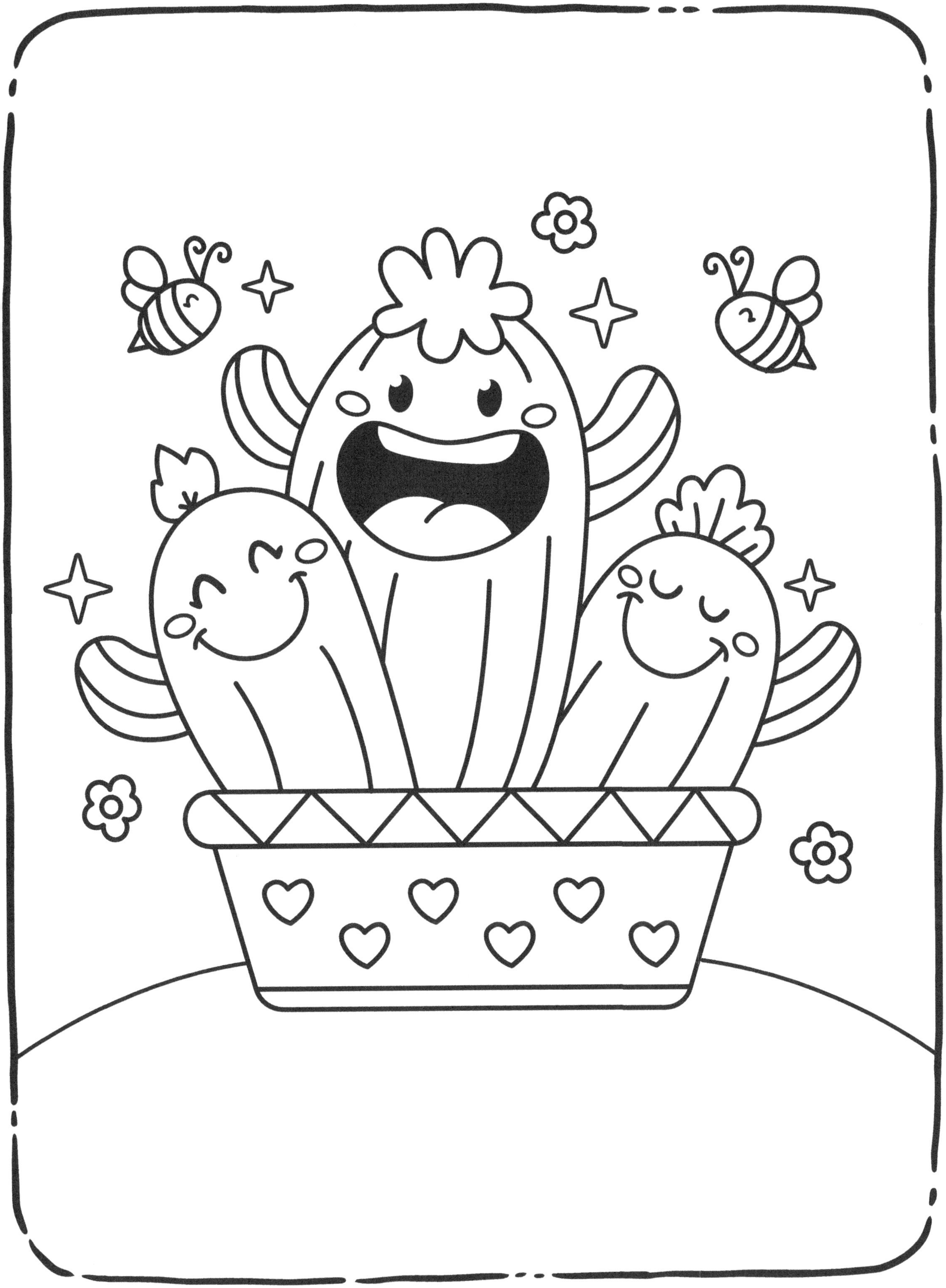

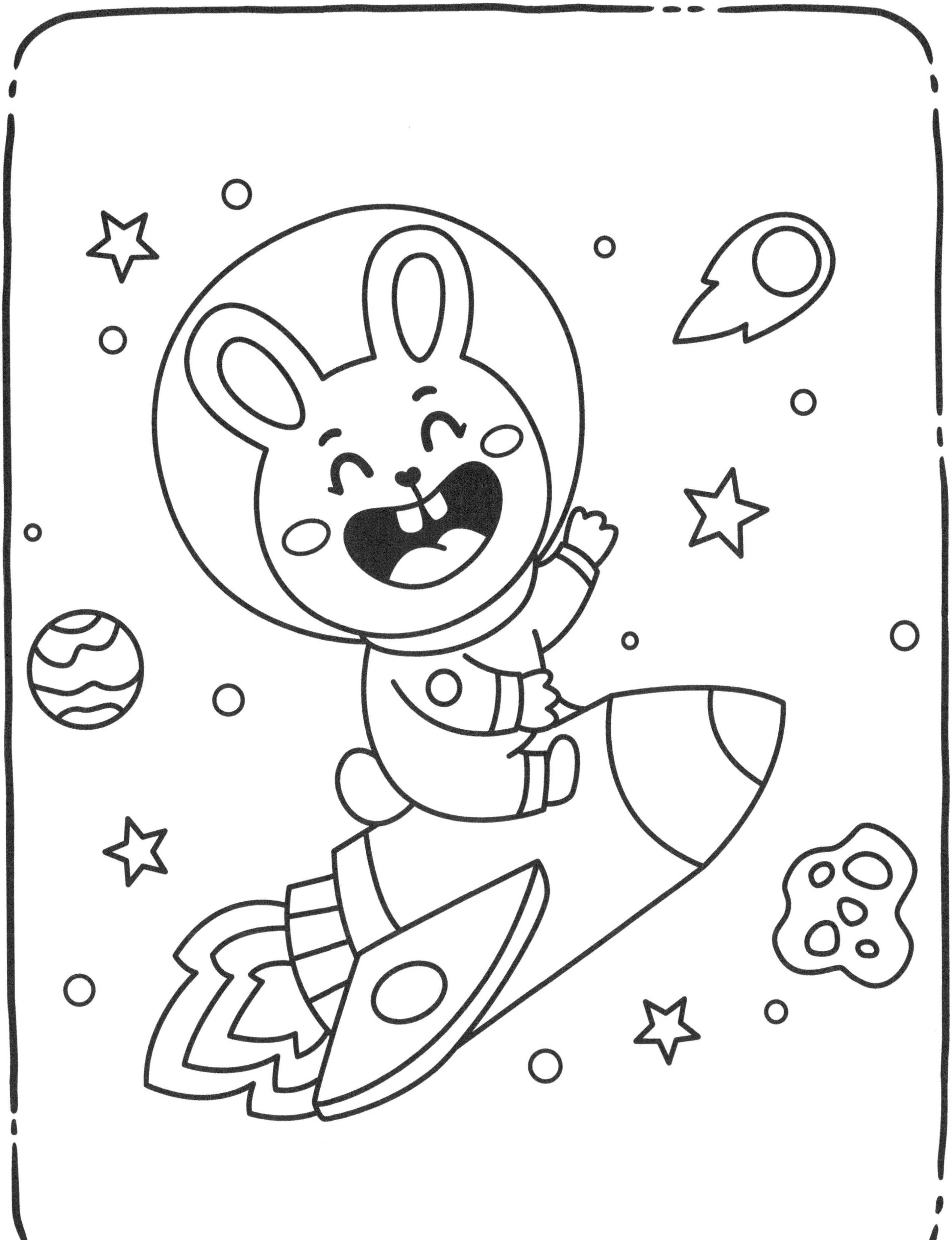

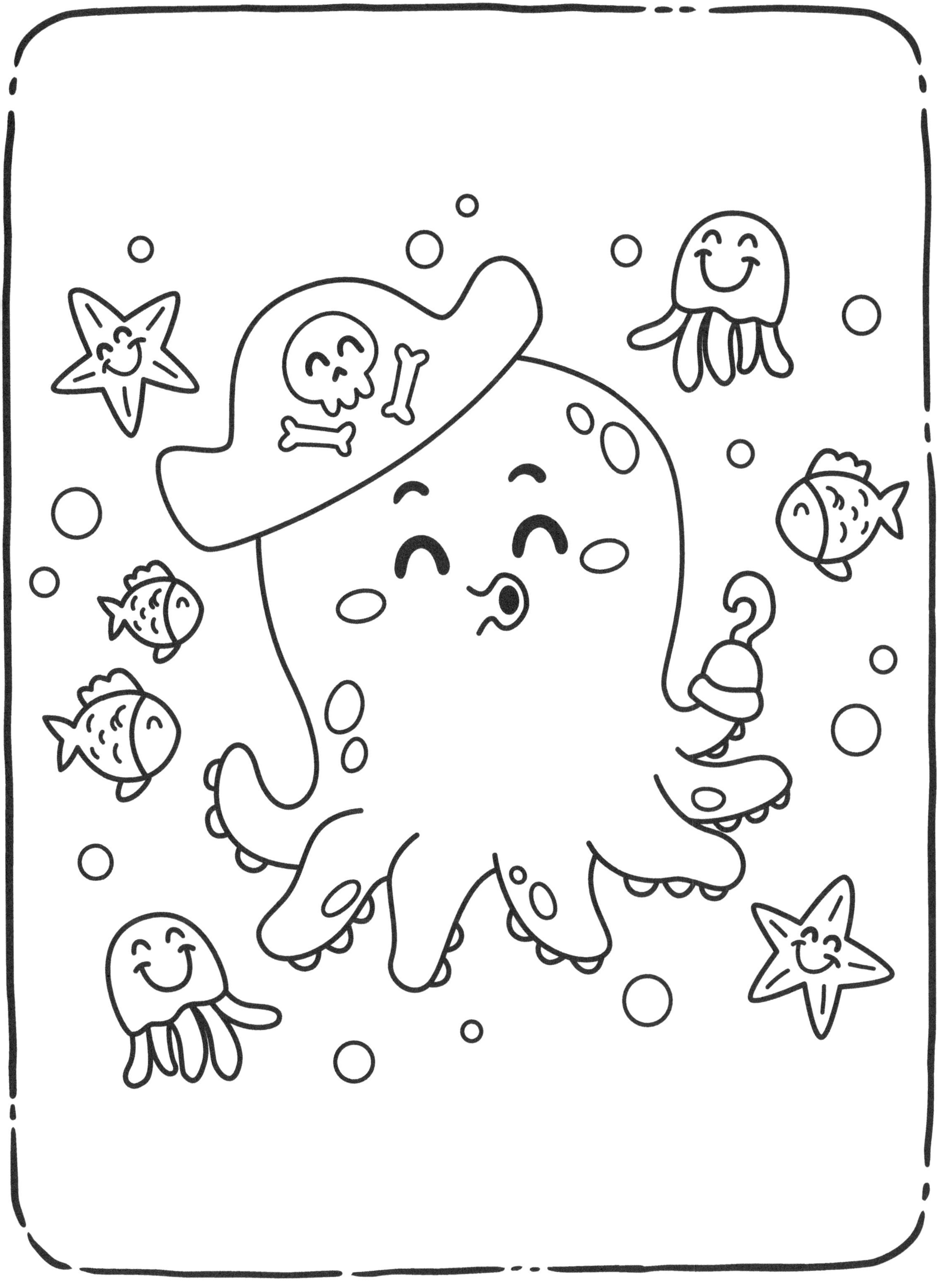

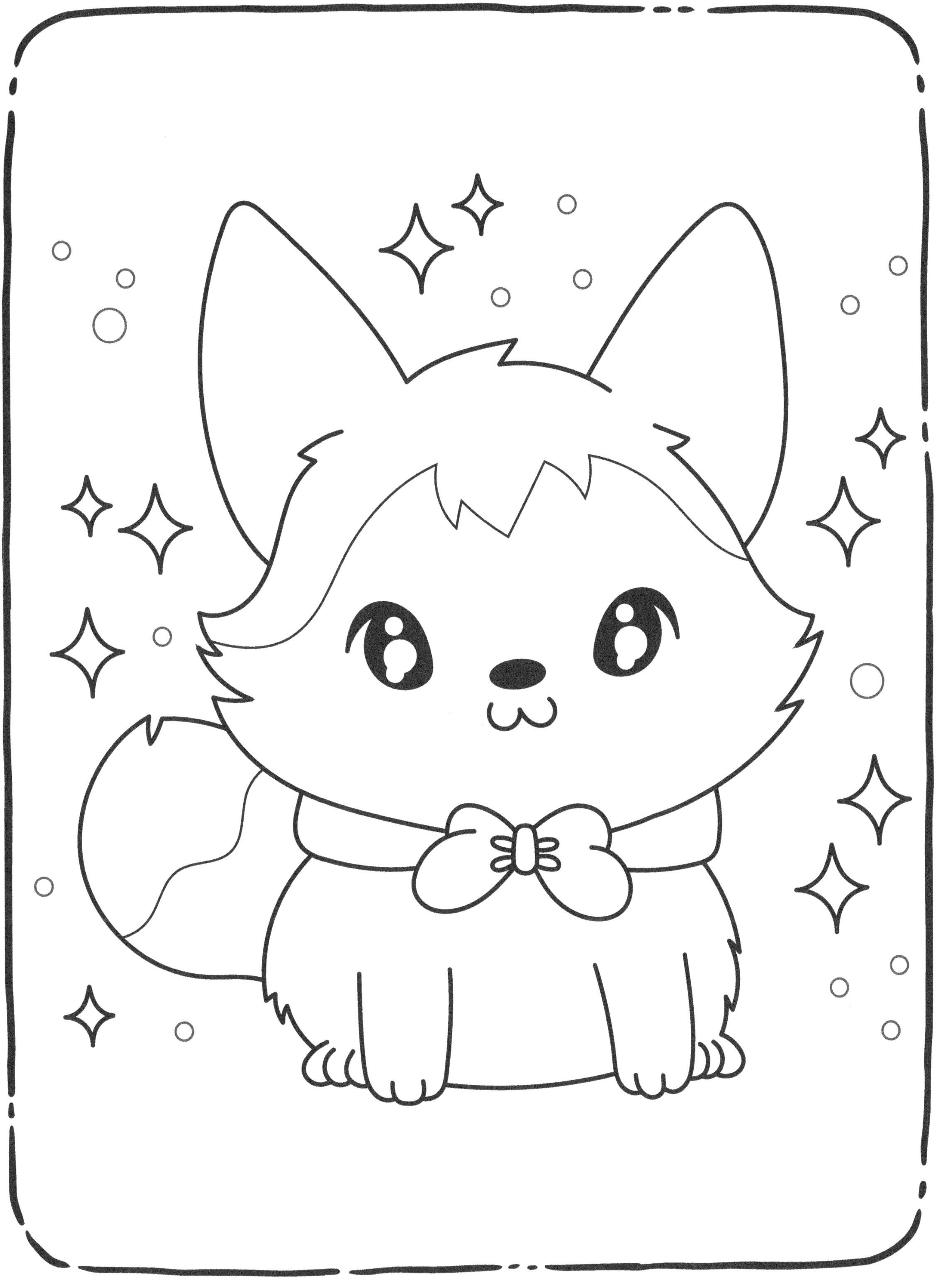

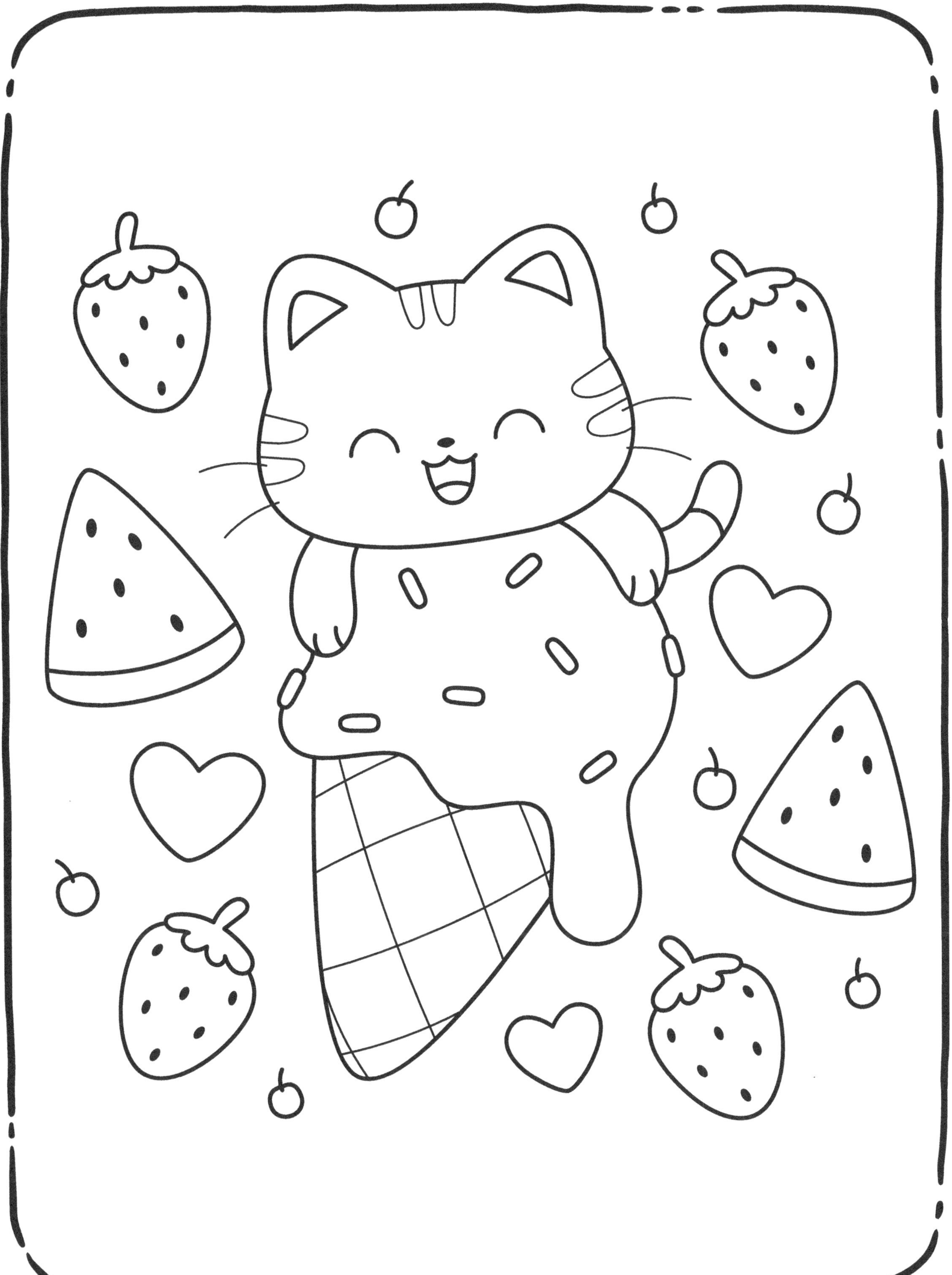

Made in the USA
Las Vegas, NV
13 March 2024

86998352R00046